To Hope —
God's Peace,
Martha Sterne

Hope Norman
from
Margaret Wade C.
Oct. 2003

Earthly Good:
Seeing Heaven on Earth

Martha Sterne

OSL Publications
Akron Ohio

Earthly Good: Seeing Heaven on Earth

ISBN 1-878009-47-8

This book is printed on acid-free paper that meets the American National Standards Institute Z39.48 Standard

Produced and manufactured in the United States of America by

OSL Publications
P. O. Box 22279
Akron Ohio 44302-0079
<www.Saint-Luke.org>

Cover design by Nancy Crouch   Photography by Margaret Bryan
The cover design features a portion of the chasuble described in "Where is God?"
It was designed by the children of St. Andrew's Episcopal Church, Maryville, Tennessee.

A version of "Door Openers," "The Gospel According to Roy," and "The Sting of Chlorine" previously appeared in the Maryville Daily Times. A version of "A Holy New Light" previously appeared in the Columbia Seminary Journal for Preaching.

The poem on page 20 is taken from "The Stars Declare His Glory" by Timothy Dudley-Smith © 1981 Hope Publishing Co., Carol Stream, IL 60188. All rights reserved. Used by permission.

The Order of Saint Luke is a religious order dedicated to sacramental and liturgical scholarship, education and practice. The purpose of the publishing ministry is to put into the hands of students and practitioners resources which have theological, historical, ecumenical and practical integrity.

for my husband, Carroll

Contents

Foreword

If you are not already sitting some place that is quiet and comfortable then you might as well go there, because once you begin reading this book it is going to be difficult for you to stop. Language like this is hard to come by, especially when it serves a vision of such unusual clarity that you don't know whether to laugh or cry at what you are suddenly able to see. As far as I know, there is no other voice in the world like Martha Sterne's. In person it is so warm and folksy that the tart insights slip right past your defenses. On the page it is so gorgeously quirky that you wonder how she learned to put words together like this, so that the most ordinary things in the world start leaking divine light.

So much devotional writing these days labors to lift us out of our humdrum existence. The idea seems to be that God has something much better in mind for us, and that if we could just concentrate a little harder then both we and those around us might be improved. Call it the spirituality of ascension. Martha Sterne's writing leads in the opposite direction. Her idea seems to be that God is right here, in all the trying circumstances of everyday life on earth, and that the only thing required of us is to trust that enough to let our love loose on this bent world the same way God does. In her wise, funny and utterly candid hands, nothing remains trivial. A cigarette ash is all she needs to proclaim death and resurrection. A can of Coke becomes a sacrament of communion. Call it the spirituality of incarnation.

For all the heart in this book, there is no sentimentality, and for all the faith in it there are no clichés. Read it long enough and you may discover that Martha Sterne is contagious. Before you know it, you are talking like her and thinking like her, be- cause the way she sees the world is the way you want to see it too: full of earthly good, and shot through with inexhaustible grace.

Barbara Brown Taylor

Prologue

One warm summer morning lots of years ago, I was going through the motions of monthly communion with about a dozen very old people in a nursing home in Atlanta. I had forgotten about the service and rushed over, a little resentfully, from the busy urban parish where I served.

Everybody had already been wheeled into a circle in the sunroom and some people dozed and some held onto their closed prayer books and a few stared off into space. The sunroom had large wire cages with yellow canaries and little tiny blue or pink birds who took quick flights inside their cages and chirped sometimes in unison, though they settled down to silence once we got going.

I droned through the words of the service and when we got to the Lord's Prayer, almost everybody chimed in, as usual, because the familiar words caught hold somewhere and, as usual, I thought, that's nice.

Then came the giving out of the bread and wine. I moved around the circle with the bread and some people took the bread in their hands and others opened their mouths like little birds and sometimes they forgot to chew until one of the attendants reminded them, Honey, want to chew that there up? And I got to a woman who had seemed totally absent from us—staring beyond us all, burning a hole in the wall with her pale blue eyes. I moved in front of her and as my hand with the bread moved toward her face, she turned her eyes up to mine, reached out, took my hand in her hand, and guided my hand to her mouth. Our eyes were locked, and I believed she was going to kiss my hand.

She bit me. Hard. I squealed in shock and looked at my hand with the little tooth-shaped indentions already beginning to turn pink. I was amazed.

I didn't know she was there, if you know what I mean. I still don't know from whence came the bite. Was she angry about breakfast? Was it a political statement since she'd never bitten my male colleagues? Was she depressed about the aging and the caging of her ancient body as the clock ran down? Who knows?

Or maybe by the grace of God, she just decided to remind me, for God's sake, to Pay Attention. You're in a holy moment here. The Word is still becoming flesh all around you, still full of grace and truth. Pay Attention, for God's sake and for your own.

I offer you these little essays as an invitation to pay attention. Pay attention to the often ridiculous and sometimes tragic predicaments of biblical proportions that we get ourselves into, for God is there in the mess. Pay attention to the truth and beauty of other people who are so often prophets and angels in disguise. And pay attention to the nips and taps and caresses of the Spirit which over and around us lies.

I thank God for the people who have been my teachers of the Word becoming Flesh, especially the congregations of St. Andrew's Episcopal Church in Maryville, Tennessee, All Saints' Church, and St. Anne's Church, both in Atlanta, Georgia   I haven't been bitten by grace lately, but most days I keep my eyes open for the possibilities.

Holy Ground

Holy Ground

Now Moses was keeping the flock of his father-in-law, Jethro, the priest of Midian, and he led the flock to the west side of the wilderness and came to Horeb, the mountain of God. And the angel of the Lord appeared to him in a flame of fire out of the midst of a bush; and he looked, and lo, the bush was burning, yet it was not consumed. And Moses said, "I will turn aside and see this great sight, why the bush is not burnt." When the Lord saw that he turned aside to see, God called to him out of the bush, "Moses, Moses!" and he said, "Here am I." Then he said, "Do not come near, put off your shoes from your feet, for the place on which you are standing is holy ground." Exodus 3:1 - 5

Holy ground. I bet Moses was surprised. There he was on a regular kind of day, just trudging around with the sheep. All of a sudden he is standing on holy ground. And the next thing he knows God is talking to him. And the next thing after that God is talking through him. First to the children in bondage and then to Pharaoh. And the rest is, as they say, history.

This all starts when he realizes that the plain old ordinary, on-the-job ground he walks is holy. The job site is holy. The route—be it walked on red clay or sandy desert or river or even asphalt—has holy possibilities. Which is to say, God could be near. Which is to say that God might be wanting to speak to us. Or through us.

Most of the time I am oblivious to what I am standing on. I forget that wherever we stand is always holy ground because surely God could be near. I believe most of us are oblivious on most of our days, which is too bad. Because when you know that where you stand is holy, then you know that your life is full of possibilities, full of gifts to be given and received.

One morning in Atlanta I locked my car keys in the house and myself out of the house. My boss sort of liked us to come on to work regardless of the inconvenience, so I asked my neighbors for a ride to Roswell Road and caught the #5. The bus was about half full—all sorts and conditions—quiet and closed in on themselves like people are on a bus. Each of us was on the way to somewhere else, locked in our own little spaces, oblivious to the others.

The bus stopped in front of the Kroger shopping center and on stepped two bag boys whom I have seen in the store and classified as mentally challenged. I noticed that the driver, a no-nonsense looking black woman, waited until they were seated instead of pulling out as soon as the doors closed. "Well, that was nice," I thought. "I'll hand it to MARTA." A few stops down, three women, who also appeared to have fairly severe mental limits, shuffled on and sat together on one of the side-facing benches up front. For the second time the driver waited.

The three women said, "Hey" to two people on the bench across from them, an old man and a young girl who were holding hands. The man showed everybody some cross-stitch he was sewing. He never spoke a word, but he took it in that they pronounced it good. I thought at first that the young girl was a social worker who was taking the old man on an outing until she began to speak in a high voice, slurring her words. She told the front of the bus about a show on TV telling the story of one of the Kennedy children who was different. Then she looked at the old man whom I thought she was with and said, "Tell me your name again. I just can't keep hold of your name." And they giggled, all five of them.

We rolled on. One of the bag boys told us about a bird who nests in the big 'O' of the Kroger sign. The shuffling women liked that a lot. They wondered where else wonderful one might find birds' nests. And we all thought about that for a while. We also, with some gentle prodding, noted a climbing rose at a filling station and a fine baby on a bicycle seat.

I thought, I am on a bus half-full of 'retarded' people. And what is strange is that I can't figure out which half is retarded: the half that we all say are retarded or the half who have forgotten to look and smell and laugh and wonder at the grace and beauty of the world going by. Surely those who know that they are on holy ground are the ones who are human beings at full stretch, reaching out to receive the gifts of God.

I still do not have a clue as to why all those specially gifted persons were on that bus. They did not get on at the same place. As we moved into Buckhead, I noticed that the driver started calling out the stops. Sure enough, the two bag boys got off. To a group home? After they got off, the driver quit calling the stops.

Earthly Good

Most of the rest of us, including the old man and the girl and the three shuffling women, rode to the end of the line at the Lindbergh train station. I wanted to say something to the bus driver like, "Thank you for being a loving and thoughtful human being. I believe you are a shepherd in disguise as a bus driver." But I didn't say anything. I lost sight of all of them as we moved to the trains but I cannot get them out of my mind.

I thank God for those among us who give us the gift of reminding us that we stand indeed on holy ground. You know who you are. You tend to be babies or old people or sick people or lovers or anybody else who is swept up in the beauty and fragility and holiness of the world God has given to us. Thank you for telling us to take off our shoes and walk slowly.

Wondrous Love

But [Jesus] looked at them and said, "What then does this text mean: 'The stone that the builders rejected has become the cornerstone'?"
Luke 20:17 NRSV

What wondrous love is this?

You say, I am not big enough or deep enough to see the love of God. How can I see the love of God with my small eyes, my shortsightedness? Tell me, what does the love of God look like?

What does love look like? Really. You have seen love. Given love. Wanted love. So what does the wondrous love of God look like?

When Michelangelo was a very young man—twenty, twenty-one, twenty-two—he had a vision of the love of God. He went into the mountains and found the most pure, white, beautiful stone that you have ever seen. He took the marble and carved in ecstasy, enthralled with the stone's purity and beauty. There, hidden in the stone, he found his vision of wondrous love.

7

Perhaps you have seen it, the *Pieta* in St. Peter's. The perfect picture of perfect grief. The mother Mary holds her dead son across her lap, in exquisite composition; the marble folds of her garments and his loincloth are delicate, elegant, perfect. Her face, resigned and gentle, is still lovely, not etched by age and grief even in that dark hour. Jesus, too, is unbearably beautiful, stretched out as if still warm and limber, perfect and perfectly still, as if the pulse in his ankles and wrists and neck had just stopped beating. What wondrous love is this—the mother for her son, the son for us—and we are caught up in it by such wondrous beauty gleaming before us, a moment of perfect love, composed and ordered and complete.

The *Pieta* is the only piece Michelangelo signed. He was twenty-four years old, maybe to his mind at the peak of his powers. The *Pieta* was installed in St. Peter's and has enraptured crowds from that day to this. Surely Michelangelo knew that God had given him the grace to create for us perfection, deeply human, deeply divine, capturing the wondrous love and the passion of God.

Then, after a long time, oh, fifty years later, Michelangelo came back to the *pieta* image. An old man now, perhaps carving for his own tomb, but surely carving out of the living of long rich years. A master, but bent over now, arthritic, tired.

This time he used a piece of stone that had been lying around for decades, slightly gray, mottled, with shadows inside. As always, he prayed for the stone to reveal its truth and then he picked up the mallet and the chisels and began to work, breaking through the stone, chiseling away the excess, carving, cutting, moving toward its truth, trying to find the perfection.

8

And then he quit—for a month, a season—but always drawn back, coming back to the mottled stone, the stone with the shadows.

Only this time his vision of perfect love didn't look so perfect. The mother almost crouches behind the son. She is somehow awkward, trying to hold him up. He is collapsed this time, his body not resting in death, but twisted, contorted. A hooded old man—the carver?—leans over them both, the mother and the son, and another figure hangs oddly on to Jesus' side. It is hard to tell, with all the arms, it is very hard to tell who is holding up whom.

The months and years went by, and the carver kept returning, banging away at the truth, trying to find the perfection which he thought would point toward perfect love. He hammered and chiseled and cut until one day he struck a mighty blow and shattered the leg of the Body of Christ. And in a fury and in disgust at himself and his failure to capture the perfect vision, he defaced the stone, covered it up and hobbled away. Furious, for he has missed the perfection and left the mottled stone flawed and unfinished, to his mind, with the truth and the love still hidden in its shadows.

I saw his flawed *Pieta*. And I know that it is not complete. Not beautiful, really, not well composed, the human figures unfinished with proportions askew. They're still trapped in the marble, with crosshatches in the folds of their clothes and the features of their faces still veiled in stone. Not perfect, nowhere near perfection. Because what we are left with is the stone rejected.

Earthly Good

But maybe what we are left with—this rejected stone—is closer to us, gathered together in awkward humility, weak and confused. Maybe what we are left with is us, awkwardly, randomly, somehow miraculously hanging on to the Body of Christ. Hanging on for dear life to this Body, to the chief cornerstone of our faith. Broken. For us.

I saw Michelangelo's flawed *Pieta*. And the perfect one. Surely that which is perfect does reflect the love of God. But, thanks be to God, so does the flawed. The haphazard. The mottled. The unfinished. The rejected. Thank God, because look at us. At the shadows, at the fractures. Look at yourself and the others in your life. All flawed and unfinished. A perfectionist would reject every one of us. And yet all of us are where the perfect passion and the perfect love of God lurk.

What wondrous love is this?

Birthing Babies

Our friend Julia helps babies be born. Wouldn't that be a wondrous way to spend your time? Actually we all have spent our time that way at least once—every one of us—because, of course, every one of us has been there and done that. Every one of us, born of a mother and making that once-in-a-lifetime long or short, dreamy journey into this old world. Did you think that just your mama and the doctor birthed you? No, you were part of the team. You were not in suspended animation like Sleeping Beauty waiting to be rescued. You were there, too, weren't you, and you did your best to be born, to come to the dance of all creation, dressed in your finest (after all, what could be finer than your God-given birthday suit?). So you were part of the team—just a few years ago or many, many decades ago. No matter. Here you are and isn't that glorious?

Did you know that on the day (or, more likely, the night) of your birth, you'd already been sleeping and waking for a good while, working some with the rhythms of your mother but also probably already choosing your own timing. Already figuring out how to be yourself—wiggling and moving and waking up and thrilling your parents and also practicing how to drive them crazy. (Which we all do, from time to time.)

And you'd already been hearing. Oh, you knew the voices of love already. Isn't that a gift?

And you'd already been practicing breathing, oh, for two or three months, just getting the hang of it. Not with air, of course, but you just sort of practiced breathing in and breathing out— just like every creature did in the very beginning—breathing in and out the waters of creation.

In the womb, all was warm and familiar and you were sur-rounded and safe. But one day, it's time. Some chemicals change in your mother, in you, and that which is safe and warm and familiar becomes binding, and constricting; your world is too small and it's time. Not by the clock, but by the waltz of hor-mones and the music of the stars and the heartbeat of the Universe. It's time.

So you do your part. I've always thought of birthing as sort of the mother's deal and whoever—daddy or midwife or doctor or cabdriver or nurse or innkeeper or shepherd or wise man— whoever happens to be around, but then too, you do a lot. You wiggle around just right, you tuck your head just so, and you move toward freedom, toward selfhood, toward being a human being—flawed and foolish sometimes, but full of possibilities for courage and faith and hope and repentance and creation and love. You move toward life. Because, after all, you are made in the image of the Living God.

You know, Julia says we're pretty much alike. When we come into this old world, you can't tell us much apart. You can't tell what race we are—or what our daddies and mamas do for a living or whether we'll be Einstein or Groucho Marx or Mother Theresa or Donald Trump. We're all just kind of purple and a little dazed, like people arriving from a long trip—which we are, of course. And then we breathe. Julia says really, it is the breath of God right before her eyes. We breathe and—in a flash —turn all rosy and flushed with life. Isn't that a miracle? And there we are in the fullness of our being. Julia says you can see right down into our souls—no masks, no armor, no artifice. We've never been hurt or disappointed or sinful. We've never even been away from our mamas. And there we are, ready for the dance.

Julia says even there, even at the beginning, there are bright questions burning in the depths of us, clear as day. Now what? Now who? Now how? Now why? Even there at the beginning, we are little seekers. For the truth. For the beauty. And most of all we are seekers for Love.

Julia says it's funny. The first thing the mama usually does—and the daddy—is simply look. Just look. Because the baby is so amazing. Because the baby—any baby—is, dare we say, holy. Or, as William Wordsworth says, the baby, any baby, is trailing clouds of glory. Do you remember that you did that? You trailed clouds of glory into the first moment you were born.

Then, after looking in awe and wonder, the mama touches— maybe the chest, or the little fingers or the chubby toes, and then the face. Such a wonder—that which was in her all that time—now so holy and alive with possibilities. For beauty. For truth. And most of all for Love.

On that holy night when Jesus was born, the amazing thing isn't that God did anything so different. No, little brothers and little sisters of the Prince of Peace, what we celebrate is that God did

Earthly Good

something so, so ordinary. God was born, just like you, just like me. Through one of us, to all of us. The creator of all the starry nights and all the seas that ever ebbed and flowed and all the energy that ever skittered around the universe came to be born among us. To be a seeker with us. Love came to seek among us. God was born for Love.

> Silent Night, holy night.
> Son of God, Love's pure light
> Radiant beams from thy holy face
> With the dawn of redeeming grace.
> Jesus, Lord at thy birth. Jesus, Lord at thy birth.

Foundations

Jesus stopped walking. Thought a minute. Looked around at them. Presented the question, man to man, friend to friend. Look, he said, who do they say that I am? What do the people say about the Son of Man? What do the folks say about me? A prophet come again? Oh. One of the big ones, huh? The Baptizer? Hmmm. Elijah? Jeremiah? Uhuh.

Jesus said, well then. All right then, but who do you say that I am? And Simon Peter said, You are the son of the living God.

And Jesus stood for a long while and looked at his friend. And said, Bless you. You are my rock.

And Jesus grinned at the others. As if to say, believe it or not—because, of course, they all know Peter—believe it or not, he got it. He's right. The Son of Man (which is, by the way, Jesus' favorite name for himself) is the Son of God. And Jesus said I am going to build what we are about on the rock of this recognition. And nothing, not even Hell, will prevail against this rock.

And everybody smiled and nodded. Because when you love people but you don't know what in the world they're talking about, what else do you do?

Rock to build on was sort of a missing element where I grew up. There was some kind of funny clay—Yazoo, I think—that ran under most of the soil in Jackson, Mississippi. And every season, the clay would move a little and the ground would shift. Cracks would mosey up the walls and across the ceiling and sometimes up the bricks outside.

My parents' friend, Skeets, was an engineer. He was a gentle, kind man with a weathered Mississippi face, seamed usually in smiles. Only sometimes Skeets would be out in somebody's yard with his head tilted sympathetically, brow furrowed, and maybe he'd be patting the homeowner in a com- forting way. It usually meant the dreaded word had been spoken. "Foundation." Well, really the dreaded two words. "Foundation trouble."

"Foundation trouble" meant those people had to do some- thing about their foundation. Because, of course, your home just has to have a foundation to hold together. Where you live, really live, just has to be solid to last. To endure. And when you don't have real solid rock to build on, you need to make do with the materials at hand.

I was twenty-five years old before I realized most people in the world don't have their houses on jacks like we did in my hometown. It made every foundation sort of a work in progress, but when the living room went south during the winter or the kitchen went west in the spring, somebody could slide around under the house and crank the jacks up or down and sort of point all the rooms in the house back toward each other.

The older I get, the more I wonder does anybody, even God, really build anything on a solid foundation? Take the universe. So God builds a universe. Creates a universe. Not out of solid rock, oh my, no. Instead God said 'let there be' and out of the chaos and nothingness at hand came light upon light, world upon world upon world. Out of chaos and vacuum. And it was good.

And then our world, and surely others, bearing mute witness to an immense mystery. So in maybe many worlds, as on this earth, in the swirling beauty and mystery of our becoming, amidst profound heat and light and great weight and springs of water, amidst all the materials at hand, God made a home. For us here, the great round earth over, shifting and gliding and folding into itself, erupting over here, swallowing itself there. Our God-graced home, from the beginning, remaking itself over and over. Even its most rock-solid self, always and ever being re-created from the heat and the light and the great weights of ice and earth and the springs of water.

Now if God so made even the foundations of the world out of that which shifts and glides and folds into itself, then what does that say about God? And who God makes us to be?

Like Paul says, I don't have the mind to know or the words to say and none of us has the ears to hear the riches and wisdom and knowledge of God, but maybe if we recognize what Peter recognized, there are some hints and possibilities.

Earthly Good

First, remember what, through the grace of God, Peter recognized. That the Son of Man is the Son of God. Now look around you and think about that. God loves us so much that God gave his only begotten son, not to coldly observe and judge us as an alien but to be one of us. So nothing—no fear, no pain, no joy—in your life or mine is alien to God because the Child of God became the Child of human beings. And that matters a lot because when we know that kind of love, the children of human beings can become the Children of God.

Second, God speaks to us most clearly—not like Cecil B. DeMille and the big booming commandment—but God speaks to us most powerfully through the human question. Jesus does not tell but asks, calling to the depths of Peter—and the others and you and me and asking, "Listen, who do you say that I am?" Evocative, not declarative. Because in any relationship, the foundational rock of trust is created—not by insisting to each other on who we are—but by evoking from each other who we are.

✓ Listen to Dag Hammarskjöld:

I don't know Who—or What—put the question, I don't know when it was put. I don't even remember answering. But at some moment I did answer Yes to Someone—or Something—and from that hour I was certain that existence is meaningful and that, therefore, my life, in self-surrender, had a goal.

Peter knew that hour. When he stopped to listen to the question of God, when he stopped to listen to the depth of God calling to the depth of us. The Child of God to the Child of Man. Calling to each other. Recognizing each other. Shifting, gliding, emerging through the God-given grace of each other. So as

18

always, always happens when we really see each other, Jesus and Peter, transforming each other. And in that moment of recognition, the bedrock of the faith is formed. The Son of Man is the Son of God.

Finally, the moment didn't last. They never do, do they? A couple of hours later, Jesus began to tell them how he thought this thing would play itself out. In Jerusalem. In death. And in new life. Peter doesn't get it at all. God forbid, he says. This must never happen to you, he says.

And of course when the Passion comes to pass, the same Rock who said, Ah, you are the Son of the living God, whimpers, Well, really, I never knew the man.

That's the rock from which we are hewn. That's the human condition. Sometimes we get it so deep. So splendid. And the next thing you know, we are whimpering alone and ashamed in the dark.

Somehow, we know that our foundation better be stronger than we are. Because every day of our lives, if we're honest, we need jacking up or jacking down, to get pointed toward ourselves, toward each other, toward the One who made us.

I imagine Skeets when he'd give the bad news. Oh, he'd tell the truth. He'd tell you, you're in big trouble. You've got some foundation work to do and you'll have to keep doing it from now on. But then the other thing is, Skeets would stick around to work it out.

And here we are—in a slippery-slidey, swirling world created by a God who is a surprise and loves surprises. A God who makes us—and even rocks—as works in progress out of the materials at hand, out of that which sometimes cracks and crumbles and fails, in the pressure and heat and light of all that lives. But a God who chooses to stick around, to work it out, and to journey with us, the materials at hand, to work with us, toward all of us being beautiful and splendid and strong and holy and beloved and true. Toward all of us being One.

> *So order too this life of mine, direct it all my days;*
> *the meditations of my heart be innocence and praise,*
> *my rock and my redeeming Lord, in all my words and ways.*

Timothy Dudley-Smith

The Gospel According to Roy

"But a Samaritan while traveling came near him; and when he saw him, he was moved with pity. He went to him and bandaged his wounds, having poured oil and wine on them. Then he put him on his own animal, brought him to an inn, and took care of him. The next day he took out two denarii, gave them to the innkeeper, and said, 'Take care of him; and when I come back, I will repay you whatever more you spend.' Whch of these three, do you think, was a neighbor to the man who fell into the hands of the robbers?"

Luke 10:33-36 NRSV

One of my regular hangouts in our old hometown of Atlanta was the neighborhood paint and body shop. On a summer afternoon a while back, I was sitting around in their dusty little office, waiting for the latest Sterne family estimate and reminiscing with Roy, who fills out the paperwork. My ill-fated left turns. The headlight crunches, the side-swipes. The time our daughter bumped some Salvadoran immigrants who could not have been more pleasant about it. The time our son ran the car into the house. The smoldering fury of our insurance agent, a childhood friend of my husband's, thank God, and so stuck with us. I breathe a sigh of thanksgiving that through the years it's all been pretty minor and say, "Roy, you see a lot come through here, don't you?"

He nods. "I see them come and I see them go. And come back. And people get upset, you know. It really don't matter if the wreck's your fault, if the wreck ain't your fault. Wrecks are upsetting business." A fact I knew, more than I wanted to.

We nod some more. Roy thinks. His old hooded eyes get a far away look. He says, "I still remember one lady, must have been twenty years ago. She did what I believe all y'all want to do. She laid right down, right out there on the asphalt. And she hollered."

I can picture her quite effortlessly. Then I say, "What did you do?"

Roy thinks. "Well, we picked her up."

Somebody picked her up. Which is the faithful vocation, no matter where you get your paycheck. To pick up the over-whelmed, the dazed, the assaulted, the broken-spirited, the broken-hearted, the wrecked. Our vocation, our work is the practice of compassion, of showing mercy. Our job is to love our neighbor which means to act as neighbor, no matter how you feel or don't feel.

This picking up starts early. It is the first reality of human experience. Every one of us—before the beauty or the degrees or the wealth or the good works, before all of that—for every one of us, while we were yet wallowing in the mess of afterbirth, somebody figured that we were worth picking up. Somebody acted the neighbor. And from that moment on our most holy work is to be about the business of returning the favor. Back and forth, around and around, picking another up, being lifted up yourself.

When all is said and done, what we mainly do that truly matters in our lives is to practice the art of picking people up. That's the way we can thank and honor the One who made us all, by stretching out our arms wider and stronger. Who needs to be picked up in your life? And for God's sake, if it's you, lay down on the asphalt and holler.

Baptism

And just as Jesus was coming up out of the water, he saw. . . And he heard . . . "Beloved."

When I was a little girl in Mississippi, I saw a lake baptism. It wasn't a crystal clear mountain lake or a big majestic body of water like one of the TVA loops on the Tennessee River. Instead that baptism back in Mississippi was in a lukewarm, muddy pond near my grandfather's house. There were cows wading and mooing and dogs chasing the ducks and an old hateful goose that lived forever and haunted my childhood, chasing the dogs and the children and anybody else who got in her way. And there were big turtles sunning themselves on a tree long fallen into the water and bream rising to feed on the surface. It was, that little muddy pond, a place as familiar as my family's faces. Familiar and beloved—not at all a place of mystery. I would not have called it a holy place, just beloved, just part of home and yet who knows what possibilities for holiness lay hidden even in the familiar.

That August day a neighboring church was there at the pond, probably fifty people and three candidates all dressed in

Earthly Good

white—bed sheets, I believe. The preacher was in white, too, and stood in water waist deep, right where we like to water our ponies and try to make them swim us out into the middle. But now the tall preacher's there and, raising his arms, he singsong-hollers to the congregation, who singsongs back, praising God halleluia. And they all sing a long time, waves of sound, rolling off the pond. And they sing and sing and sing the new ones into the water one by one. They wade in the mud and the dung toward the preacher who takes them strong in his long arms—still singing—and wails them down into the waters. In the name of the Father and Jesus the Son and oh the Holy Ghost. Amen and amen. Let the people say amen.

I stood that day under live oaks with the moss hanging down between them and me and watched. The deep chasm of race hung between us, too. I still see them, shimmering in the heat, all around that little nothing no-name pond. I see it all, all of them, all of us, made holy—the people and the water—in the name of the Father and of the Son and of the Holy Spirit. And something broke open for me that day, an epiphany for me, that day of truth and grace, come to dwell among us with the cows and the turtles and the bream and even a snake or two. Over and over a new thing springs forth, a new heaven, new earth. From the depths of the ordinary, a new life is born. In us. Among us.

No telling what happened to those folks who were baptized in that muddy pond back in Mississippi so long ago. It was the early sixties. Brave and faithful people got in a lot of trouble back then, just by being brave and faithful. So no telling what happened to those folks baptized that day. Just like no telling where any of our paths will lead. We all have chances to be brave and to be faithful and to love God and our neighbors every day. So no telling what will happen.

But what we do know, what is our sure and certain hope, is this: it doesn't matter where your path leads. You are made in the image of God. Know that.   And you are beloved. You are worth the love of God. Trust that. Live that. And spread that around. On your ordinary days and your extraordinary ones, in the best of times and the worst.

We are beloved. We belong to Christ. And Christ belongs to God. Beloved. This day and into eternity.

Creation and the Deep

In the beginning—though a long while after the *very* beginning—after all was without form and void, after darkness covered the abyss, after God said let there be light and the heavens exploded forth to declare God's glory—a long while after the *very* beginning, in that time without time a new world was birthed in violence, wrenched from the side of the newborn sun.

And the new earth went spinning through the deep of the universe. It rushed through space, all vapors and gases like filmy long scarves, whirling and swirling—heat and chaos and steamy vacuum. And then, in that time without time, the new earth began to cool ever so slowly. And eon by eon, spinning in thick cloud and heat and dark, some of what was swirling began to sink and liquefy, and then to gather itself in slow molten waves of stuff rolling all around the globe. Gathering and rolling in endless enormous tides of primal matter that swept the earth in gloom and dark. The moon, some say, was a molten tide that just let go and poured out into the abyss.

The waves kept on roiling and rolling, then cooler and cooler and slower and slower. The wildest wandering over, the surface drying and wrinkling into mountains and valleys. The first dry land appears and the cool wind of God sweeps over the face of it all. So, now, cool enough for water. Cool enough for rain. The clouds cover this first young face of the planet and it rains without ceasing—days raining into months, into years, pouring into centuries. The waters fill the gashes and the deep ragged valleys so that now water-waves move and dance to the rhythm of their sister moon. And God calls the waters the Sea and proclaims it good. And then from the sea came the most profound miracle. From the sea, from the deep, there came the miracle of life. . . .

That is the way I picture the first creation story, thanks to the poet of Genesis and his granddaughter, Rachel Carson.

The audacious, bewildering, really absurd claim of our faith is that the same One who spoke a word out of nothing—*ex nihilo*—the One who spoke a Word and spilled forth a universe full of the mystery of stars and moons and seas, the One who caused light to shine into the sea and brought forth life from the deep—that same Power and Glory has come to us. Come into time and space to be with us, to speak the Word of new creation, new life to us.

And so another creation story. This time a homely scene. Ordinary. Weary, haggard men cleaning nets, moving slow in the early morning light by the sea after a long night. Exhausted. With empty nets. And not for the first time. Not by a long shot. But, like you do, they had learned to live with sometimes empty and just plod on.

They—Peter and Andrew and the others—had learned to live with the way things are. Which means mostly to settle for less, and sometimes to settle for nothing. To get by. Because that's the way things are. All us grownups know that. Gone are the wild, free-floating dreams of youth. You eke along. Sometimes you catch a few. And sometimes you come back with empty nets. All in all, you get along. But you fish close to shore because close to shore, you may not catch the big ones, but you figure you're safe.

So another long night with empty nets. You tie your boat. And you clean your nets. Your chapped hands move through the nets and pick out the seaweed and the shells. You plod on through the tasks almost on automatic. And just like the other empty net days, you know that soon you will turn away from the possibilities of the sea and the early morning and trudge back to narrower horizons, to your familiar little bed in your little room—to sleep the day away, perhaps to dream.

But then—right into this humdrum way-things-are little world of yours, right into your empty nets, your emptiness—a Word is spoken. *Put out into the deep.*

Your shoulders ache, and you groan inside, oh please, what now. And you think, uh-oh. And you mutter you don't want to. And you whisper that it won't work. And you shake your head and roll your eyes at the very idea of you in the deep because the deep is, well, deep. And you've always liked it close to shore where you can't get lost. And you like the shallow water because you know just where the bottom is. And you can see what you're catching. Why, cast a net into the deep and God knows what you'll get.

And the Word comes back, *Exactly.*

31

And you sigh. And you think I'm tired. I've been trying and nothing much comes of it. And you look at the ground and kick at the dust. And your shoulders sag. And you start to walk away from the Word. Then for no clear reason, just out of the blue grace of God, you say okay, I'll try again. I'll try the deep even. And you say yes. And you obey the Word that's come to you.

So you sail into the deep, whatever that looks like for you— wherever in your life it seems far from shore and the bottom is hard to see. Without much confidence you cast your empty net. You put it out there. And, lo and behold, there is a miracle. You find the deep to be the deep abundant life of God. New life, grace from the deep, to us. From the same Holy One who spoke the Word that began it all.

Strange, isn't it that new life comes to and through the ones who know the bitterness of empty nets. Abraham and Sarah are way too old to bear new life. And yet. Joseph is betrayed by his family and enslaved when God uses him to save a nation. Moses is a convicted murderer who becomes the lawgiver. Peter betrays and then becomes the rock of the church, and Paul persecutes and becomes the door. All of those people with ragged pasts and limited futures and empty nets. And now you and me.

We clean up pretty good, but let's face it. We know what it's like to come up empty.

Which is why we need God so. If you think that nothing new can happen for you, no new life, no new fullness of being, no new creation, then stop for a moment. Stop cleaning your empty nets for a minute.   And listen.

Put out into the deep. And let down your nets.

Of course, that's not the end of the story. It is genesis. Just like with Peter and Andrew, it is beginning. Remember what happens then: "and they brought their sagging boats to land and left everything and followed him."

Earthly Good

✓ *Alligators*

*Then the L*ORD* answered Job out of the whirlwind: "Where were you when I laid the foundation of the earth?" Job 38:1, 4*

My parent's biggest anniversary bash was their Golden Wedding Anniversary, back in 1991. All of our relatives and some of their oldest friends gathered out in the country outside of Natchez, Mississippi at an old place where Mother's family has been living and re-unioning for almost two hundred years now. Most of the land is deep old woods full of songbirds and wild turkey and deer. Spanish moss garlands the trees and a great blue heron sails among the ponds. You have to chase the cows out of the yard every once in a while which gives the children and dogs something to anticipate. It's really a peaceful sort of place, a kind of dark and green paradise.

It was just right for the occasion. After all, a 50th wedding anniversary is almost by definition a calm and gentle celebration. A celebration of making it, of weathering the storms, of keeping the faith through the better and the worse, and the richer and the poorer, and the sickness and the health. A sort of

Earthly Good

safe harbor time, homecoming time when people sit and maybe rock and smile and remember. And mostly that house party was safe harbor time. Except for one thing. This alligator showed up.

We had never ever had an alligator on that place. And here is this thing—eight feet long if it was an inch—steaming up and down the pond nearest the house. Sometimes just his eyes showed. And sometimes he floated way high so you could see from the tip of his snout to the end of his tail. He was huge.

Of course, immediately, the alligator experts among us emerged. Some told us how he got there. Others told us how long he could stay under water and how fast he could go on land, the consensus being that he could outrun a dog. The mothers of small children loved hearing that.

Some told us how much we could get for him per pound. One heard about the financial possibilities and hung off a tree and tried to lasso him. And then there was the expert who told us how to make him paddle over to you—just what I wanted to do, let me tell you. But, just in case you want to be able to call an alligator, here's what you do: hit the water with a stick and bark like a dog.

All in all he kind of added to the party. The Game and Fish warden said he'd come in a couple of days to trap him and take him to a new home, but then one afternoon, the alligator just disappeared—just vanished. We looked all around that pond. And into dusk-dark, different ones would go and watch out for as long as any of the experts thought he could hold his breath. He just was not anywhere to be seen. And here's something strange: if you think seeing an eight-foot-long alligator is kind of scary, try not seeing one. Terrifying. Did he crawl over to the graveyard pond where the big children jump way out into the middle on the rope swing? Or did he go the bream pond where the little ones learn how to canoe and the old people fish? Or was he lying in wait in the brush by the water where we pick blackberries? Where, oh where, were the thrashing tail, the gaping jaws, the teeth, the danger, the chaos? Was it just gone, crawled back into the mystery from whence it came?

We said he was our first alligator but he wasn't, really. I believe that most of our deepest fears are sort of alligator fears. The alligators we see—with terrifying clarity—gliding fast and hungry towards us or towards somebody we love. And the alligators we don't see—the ones holding their breath, biding their time, just under the surface, waiting in the dark and the muddy places. Some of us spend our whole lives worrying about the alligators that we don't see. And then there are those of us who just jump right into alligator-infested waters, maybe because we are careless or foolish or proud or greedy or even maybe just innocent.

The alligator—the chaos, the storm, the danger, the divorce, the illness, the crisis—and the human response—what you and I do in the midst of chaos—and the presence of God in chaos—these are profound issues of faith. And the stories about chaos and God and us are just about the holiest stories we've got. Cross-shaped, they are the heart of Scripture and the lifeblood of the church.   God's presence even at the worst of times—that's the heart of the matter. And our trust—not in ourselves but in God—is what we work out or work to avoid working out all of our lives.

Earthly Good

37

So Job. The winds blow, illnesses come, friends get self-righteous, money runs out, loved ones die. The alligators snap their jaws, bad times. And bad news, or at least hard news. The hard word comes from God and it is spoken in the middle of a storm, literally spoken by God out of the storm, out of the whirlwind. And God's hard word is that we aren't ever going to understand, much less control—not Job, not us, not Job's friends, not all the alligator experts in the world. We aren't ever going to understand and control the why and what and how of evil and suffering and chaos. That's the hard word of God in the whirlwind, in the chaos; hard news for human beings, limited, bound up creatures living not in paradise but east of Eden.

Because, after all, where were we when it all got made? The foundations of the earth and the morning stars and the wild ox and the storehouses of snow and the home of the east wind and Leviathan and the soaring hawk and the springs of the sea and the dwelling of the light and the gates of death and the gates of deep darkness. The hard news is that the Creator does not place us and our pain in the center of the universe. And we are never, ever going to control the chaos and we're never, ever going to control God, not even by doing it all right, not even by our morality, not even by our faithfulness. Job, for instance, stayed faithful through the worst that can happen. Even then he cries "For I know that my Redeemer lives, and that at the last he will stand upon the earth . . . and I shall see God and not as a stranger." Job knew that. Job said that. Job kept the faith. And he hurt bad and the chaos swirled anyway. And that seems like bad news to me.

But listen. Somewhere in the mystery of God—we don't know how, we don't know why—that hard word, that bad news, touches good news, touches gospel, touches grace. And the hard words of suffering and chaos and the gentle words of grace and deliverance are both true in a cross-shaped way that we cannot understand, but only experience. The mystery of God is that the Word of God speaks not only out of the storm but into the storm. The mystery of God is that the Word of God—hard and graceful—became flesh and dwelt among us, because God is *Emmanuel*. God is with us. And sooner or later the wind will cease. And there will be great calm.

Earthly Good

Cokes with Lillie Vidal and Biggie

My favorite house to visit, growing up, was the home of two sisters, my great aunts, Lillie Vidal and Biggie, a.k.a. Big Jo, though both of them were less than five feet tall. Four or five times a year, our car doors would slam, and they would rush out the front door to greet us, squealing and hugging and kissing, and we would head in a herd back to the kitchen to get Cokes. Then on to the dining room with some of us settling in hard, straight-backed chairs and leaning toward each other around the table, and a couple of us sprawling on a scratchy horsehair sofa full of lumps. That they had a huge and hideous sofa in their dining room just sort of added to the allure. We would sit under the portraits of some very fierce-looking ancestors and the painting of a lady swimming naked and we would hear everybody's news—all the stuff of our lives. What's the fourth grade like? Did my sister still love to dance? How is my campaign for a pony going? How much we've grown! Why we are as tall as Biggie! How is our loathsome dog, Toby? (Toby must have bit one of them once) Has anybody run over him yet? No? Too bad. I didn't say they were sweet little old ladies.   Then there would always be very big stuff to tell us back—since they were two old ladies in Natchez, Mississippi. And we would hang on every word.

Everything we talked about was always the most amazing or the most horrible or the most thrilling or the most beautiful, or the most lovely thing we will have ever heard. All the stuff of life, lifted up to admire or wonder over or fuss about or laugh about. All the stuff of life lifted up, offered to each other, not because the stuff mattered, but because we mattered, each to the other. And when we came to see those sisters, we knew we mattered. Each of us. All of us.

That's where I learned about hospitality. On State Street in Natchez from my great aunts. They were very different women: one talked and sang and made us laugh; the other, shy and gentle, mostly listened. A secretary in a bank and a clerk in an insurance company—not movers and shakers in the world—just small world makers. Shapers of a small world of free and friendly space where one could give and one could receive. Where the decor never changed except to grow shabbier and it didn't matter. Where the cuisine was, shall we say, limited, and it didn't matter. Cokes were kind of their best dish. None of that mattered because I knew I did. I mattered. I counted. That I received mattered. And that I gave mattered. And that is hospitality.

Hospitality is a profound word, a holy word and a word worth recovering because hospitality is the word for the most powerful kind of human relationship. The word comes from the Latin 'hospes', and it can mean guest or host or both. Hospital-ity, as in hospital, as in healing, as in making whole, is what happens in the between, when, as Henri Nouwen says, the space between people is free and friendly. Hospitality happens when we aren't trying to pay somebody back or make somebody have a good time or make anybody do anything. No power plays, no obligations to be fulfilled, just freedom and friendliness between the *hospes*—the guest and the host. Miracles can happen in that kind of space.

The Bible is brim-full of stories of hospitality, one of the most loved being the story in Luke's gospel about another pair of sisters. One is the drudge, scurrying around the kitchen and whining because her sister won't help her. Busy, busy with her apron on and a hot and sweaty face. Trying very hard to be hospitable and do and produce and give. And all the time the hospitality is happening somewhere else without her.

Everybody knows it's much better to be the other sister, the gentle, attentive Mary—sitting quietly with her guest—being present with her guest, as they say. In this story about hospitality, Mary is the one to be like. She's chosen the better part. And I like sitting around and being gentle and attentive to guests better than slaving in a hot kitchen anyway.

But Martha and Mary don't show the whole picture. There are as many ways to practice hospitality as there are us. Remember the Good Samaritan who doesn't just sit gently and be present to the man lying in the ditch. He does a lot of work for the man. And then remember Abraham and Sarah and the three mysterious guests who come to visit. In that story the hosts are literally running to take care of the guests. Abraham runs to greet them, rushes to get them settled in the shade. Hustles to get cool water, hastens to Sarah's tent to get her started making cakes, runs to the herd to pick out dinner. These people are

Earthly Good

working hard for their guests. Their hospitality has lots of doing and cooking and carrying on.

So why do the Good Samaritan and Sarah and Abraham come across so fine, and Martha comes across like a drudge in all her cooking and running around? Of course, if somebody is bleeding to death or hungry or thirsty, you have your hospitality mapped out for you. I think we know that. We may not always respond faithfully but we often know what the faithful response is. It's the Martha/Mary story that confuses me. Truly, I figure if you are focusing on doing for others, then everybody ought to cut you some slack. And here Jesus doesn't.

Instead Jesus listens to her and he looks at her, hot and sweaty and irritated—just like we all get when we feel like we are stuck with all the work and nobody appreciates us. And he tells her—Martha, Martha, wait a minute. Two things are going on that make hospitality—free and friendly space-making—impossible.

First it can't happen when we are distracted—even with much serving, many dishes, much hard work, much production. Sometimes that is the way for us to control the others and distance them, too. The means becomes the end and hospitality gets lost in the shuffle.

And second it can't happen when we are resentful. Martha was pulling Mary's load. 'Course it was Martha's idea to have a five course meal and if this Martha is like another Martha I know, she didn't bother to check out the plan with her sister. So she is distracted, resentful and in a great hot hurry to do many things for her guest when all he wants from her is a Coke. Or, maybe a

Coke and a tomato sandwich would be fine. When really all he wants from her is her.

Martha, Martha you are worried and distracted by many things. There is need of only one thing.

Hospitality is a holy word. In it is the only faithful possibility we Christians have of destroying our enemies. We destroy our enemy when our enemy becomes our friend. That takes free and friendly space where we both can move from defensiveness to disarmament, from fear of rejection and self-doubt and insecurity to gift-giving so that the very stuff of life is lifted up and offered and accepted back and forth just as at Lillie Vidal and Biggie's table.

And so hospitality turns out to be the way to experience the divine. Notice who all the guests are. Look at the gifts given when there is free and friendly space. To Abraham and Sarah is given the promise of new life when the three guests announce the birth of a baby. And look at the gift that Martha's guest brings—freedom from drudgery, freedom from production, freedom for simplicity. Martha, Martha, stop doling out stuff. And stop needing to be needed. Stop hiding behind your hurry and your pots and your pans and your production. You are wanted and that is better than being needed. Shh. Rest. Here, where it's free and friendly.

I believe God calls us all to be co-creators of small worlds of hospitality, as in, "where two or three are gathered . . . ." Small worlds, in the offices and the schools and at home and all the places where we are—small worlds where one is wanted as much as needed, where one can give sometimes and receive sometimes. Where one matters. Small worlds where each one matters so that we come to know that all matter.

They are dead now, Biggie and Lillie Vidal, but I still can hear their voices and their laughter and sometimes I imagine what we would be talking about now. They—rockbed Presbyterians—got over me marrying a Roman Catholic once they decided he was good-looking. And anyway, as they would say, he's ours now. So I guess they would get over me being an Episcopal priest. We would have to discuss it a lot, though. Lillie Vidal would say, "This is the most horrible thing I've ever heard." And we'd talk it all through, not because it matters, but because I matter. I miss them to this hour.

Come, risen Lord and deign to be our guest;
Nay, let us be thy guests; the feast is thine.

Circles

Where is God?

Where is God? was the question.

Where is God? she asked them, forty of the kids in our parish from eighteen months to sixteen years. Where is God? the painter asked. Tell me and we'll paint a chasuble for the priest to wear at the altar. Tell me where God is and we'll make a garment out of your telling, a garment fit to wear as we thank God for all our blessings. So tell me where God is.

They answered in crayon masterpieces and whispered stories and giggles and depth theology and even Play-doh. And they pointed to themselves, to each other, to their hearts and one two-year-old pointed to the bottom of her shoes thus echoing Paul Tillich's acclaimed assessment that God is the ground of all being.

And they said, well, God's in our hills, so she drew the hills and God's in the colors so she drew them and God's in the wind and wind is hard to draw, but she drew it. And God's in the flowers and the sun and the moon and they told her to remember the moon has different faces. One child said God is in the black holes in space, even there, and in the night and the day and somebody said, God's on Saturn, which is there somewhere on that chasuble, ringed in red.

And the glory of God, our children told us, is in the animals we love—our dogs and cats, our parrots, our ponies. Somebody said, well, don't forget God made pigs too. And woolly sheep. And in the wild, God's glory is in the wild in great apes and giraffes and butterflies and even a bat. I want to shake the hand of the kid who thought of the bat. And in the fish and in the gentle manatee.

Two boys thought to themselves, we'll draw the animals that kill, the predators, and we just bet they won't get in this where-is-God thing. But when they took the fierce drawings to the painter, she said, oh, just what I need, just right, just so. For God's glory is in the fierceness of things—they already know that, our kids, so we don't have to deny fierceness. God's glory is even in death, in the cycle and circle of life and death and life again.

And (my personal favorite) there's a snake biting a hippopotamus on the bottom and the hippo looks like he's squealing like mad. So God's in the sound of things also—our squeals of indignation and our songs and wistful murmurs and declarations of the heart. God is in it all, us all, for we are there, too, on that chasuble, filled with the glory of God—our children seem to know that we are part of the big, gracious and lively household of God.

And you know what else our children know? We are not at the center; we are just dancers in the dance. But we are the dancers who step outside the dance of creation and know, sing, paint, tell; we are the ones who step outside the dance and know the glory of God is shot through it all.

One of my parishioners told me that 'faith' had always been about doing one's duty and going to church and sitting through boring sermons and enduring pledge drives. And then one day— through the love of friends and the beauty of the world around us and the nourishment of the Body and the Blood —one day the realization came, my God, it's not me doing my duty that saves me, it's grace all over and around me—grace of God every breath, every taste, every touch. All this time 'faith' had meant being bored to death by religiosity; and instead, faith is about the glory of God dancing in all of creation. It's about the mighty grace of God relentlessly following us, leading us, through life, in death, even beyond death to new life in Christ who draws creation to himself so that at the last we are all of us, all there is, dwelling at peace in the glory of God.

So if you go to church to do your duty, forget it. The chil-dren know better. They know that the glory of God fills all of creation—the light and the dark, the gentle and the fierce, the air and the water, the cosmos and the microcosm. And that death is not the last word, glory be to God. The last word we have from God is Life. The tomb is not the end. The tomb is, in the end, finally empty. Creation dancing knows that. And we, who think we know so much and really know so little, we, through the grace of God in Christ Jesus, can know that too.

Just ask the kids where God is. Christ is risen. The Lord is risen indeed.

The Rhythm of the Spirit

My brother, Malcolm, six years younger, was a terrible pest. A tow-headed, hardheaded child, he had bluebird-blue eyes that fixed on you and while he thought up something terrible to do, he would stare at you and not blink. I mean, that kid could go hours without a single blink. He and our schnauzer, Toby, were the center of a marauding band of little boys and dogs who were usually into something untoward somewhere in the neighborhood. For instance, they went to the lake on the golf course where our parents played and fished out all the golf balls—many with names on them—and made a tidy profit selling the golf balls, 500 of them, back to their owners at my wedding reception.

Mac made it through high school somehow—he was actually pretty smart, just shiftless—and came over to Atlanta to go to Emory. My husband and I saw him when he decided to do his laundry, so at least once a semester.

He had an apartment on Waddell Street in Little Five Points, a street on which dwelled, as they say, one of everything and two of most. His next-door neighbor was a nightclub for deaf people. And so in the evenings, in the dusk-dark, people would saunter past Mac's apartment on the bumpy sidewalk. He began to love watching them—their faces lit up, their hands flashing, husky laughs perhaps never heard by the laughers' companions—they'd sashay by my brother, anticipating the dance.

Sometimes, intrigued, Mac would follow and join them in the club, to get caught up in the throbbing of drums. Always the rhythm of drums pulsing through the air, through the wooden floor, in the seats, in the throbbing tables, and the people swaying to the rhythms of unheard melodies, to the pulse and throb of them. Everybody danced together, having a grand time in a space filled with the invisible, irresistible rhythm which bound them together. A rhythm which they would never hear completely, never grasp fully, but only live and move and have their being in—the rhythm of the dance.

Well, you know where I am going. The church could do worse than be a club for the deaf, a club for the blind, a club for the voiceless, for the hungry, for the brokenhearted. We could do worse than be a people exquisitely aware of our limitations so that we are open ever wider to hearing the inexplicable grace throbbing every moment all around us, rejoicing to be enfolded in the rhythm of the spirit of the universe. The rhythm of the spirit which we call holy. On Pentecost the church gives thanks for the miracle of the spirit that binds us together and which connects us to all human beings, indeed to all there is to the furthest reaches of the universe.

I think of my brother. Now he's a balding blond guy with eyes that still pierce just behind wire-rimmed glasses. He does blink more regularly. He lives out west because he loves the mountains and cross-country skis, and he moves across state lines whenever he hears a wedding bell.

He grew up to be a doc—like our daddy and granddaddy— and he's spent most of his time with the very sickest kids. He tells me stories of the resilience of little babies and stories of the pain of losing kids and of the glory of good nurses and of the endurance of families. He knows what matters, my brother, as he journeys and guides others through those terrifying foreign countries of illness and injury and disorder.

Except for my ordinations and our father's funeral, I don't think Mac has set foot in a church since high school when he had to. I don't think God loves him any less than me or you—Jesus never said you have to go to church, rather you have to love your neighbor—but I wonder how many Macs there are out there who might be fed and given life, who don't know how real it is here with us—praying and hearing and trying to obey (which, by the way, in Hebrew are the same word—to hear is to obey). I wonder about people who don't know how earthy our mission is—caring for the weak and encouraging the fainthearted and alleviating suffering and working on a team and offering hope and finding endurance—and dealing with life and death and taking deep joy where you can find it.

My brother doesn't know how real and true and not-churchy the Body of Christ can be, and I think there are a lot of people like him. This bothers me. Does it bother you that many of our friends and brothers and sisters and sometimes our children don't see the truth and love in the church? I think there's a wake up call for us. A pentecost call. To speak a word—when someone

Earthly Good

asks—about how you experience God in us and among us and through us or what it's like for you when the Word gets spoken in the language of the heart. When you—passing all understanding—hear and know the rhythm of the beat of the peace of God.

The Narrow Door

So the question comes . . . Will only a few be saved? Maybe the questioner is just idly curious or maybe the questioner is in danger or need or fear or dire straits. And the answer comes, and it's weird—it's not really an answer to the question at all. It is not some quantity. Jesus doesn't say, well, 18% of the people will be saved or 144,000 people will be saved, as is rumored by some folks who knock on doors. And the answer is not some scientific theory either—Jesus doesn't analyze the probabilities, the chances for salvation of those other people out there. Really the answer isn't about anybody else but the questioner. The answer isn't about the few or the many or the most or the least. The answer is about the one who is standing there questioning, who could be you or me. And the answer is to strive to enter by the narrow door.

Well. Strive to enter by the narrow door. What on earth could that mean? I've got a lot of other things I'm doing right now. I'm rushing up and down the highways of my life—my family, my job or maybe my no job, my plans, my fears, my loves, my sins, my guilt, my anger, me, me, my, my life. I haven't got time to piddle around looking for some silly narrow door when I'm rushing up and down the highways of my life. I have really not got the time or energy right now to find some narrow door. I am too busy or I am too afraid or I just do not understand what on earth that means.

Houston Smith, a Christian, an old man now and deep lover of souls, has spent his whole life learning and teaching about the ways that human beings seek and are found by God. You may have seen him with Bill Moyers. He's been around everywhere. He grew up in China, the child of Christian missionaries, and immersed himself in the great religions of the East—Hinduism and Taoism and the wisdom of Confucius and the path of enlightenment that Buddha commends. Later he was taught by the Jews; as to Islam, he apprenticed himself to a Sufi master for fifteen years. He's spent close to 80 years exploring all that, and you know, the wonder is he has found so much in common, so much. Smith says that in all the great paths to God there are always these three things: always great awe and praise of God, always concern for other people, always awareness of an inner life burning inside each of us, yearning for the Holy.

My sister-in-law, Helen, has been in a group of three or four Jews and their rabbi and three or four Christians and their Presbyterian pastor that meets every week to study scripture. It's only taken them three years to steam through Genesis. They'll be in the wilderness in Exodus for God knows how long; maybe, like the children of Israel, forty years. But what she tells me is how rich the mix is, how loving the community. She tells me how refreshed she is through them each week to journey on down her own Christian path, through her own narrow door into the depths of her own gifts and needs and hopes and disciplines and ministries and faith. Which is to say her companions honor her and each other and encourage each and all to walk through his or her own narrow door into the life of God.

Strive to enter by the narrow door. The one that's just your shape—not your daddy's or your mama's, not the approved denominational shape, not your hero's shape or your most envied enemy's shape, not anybody else's shape in the whole wide world. You strive to enter by the narrow door, the one that is just your shape. On the other side is not me-centered life—so precarious—but God-centered life. It is a mystery that cannot be touched but that will touch you and me to the core, and, as Paul says, when you walk through the narrow door, you begin the removal of what is shaken, so that what cannot be shaken may remain.

Now I think a lot and pray a lot about ways that churches—my church—can have wide-open doors to invite people in and include them in a community of faith. I want us to have wide-open doors and enough room for all. But finally the broad invitation into our wide doors must at some point for each of us become deeper and, yes, narrower. At some point I hope everything we do—our prayers, our study, our ministries and outreach, our parties, our money, our friendships and our conflicts—helps to point each of us to the narrow door, the one that is just your shape or just my shape into God-centered life in which our wholeness, our salvation lies.

Will only a few be saved? That is just the wrong question. Slow down. Lift up your heart. Open your eyes. Listen. Touch. Ask. Seek. Knock. Look for the narrow door—the one that's just your size.

The Party Scene

I have never been what you would call a party animal.
Either as a guest or a hostess, I just don't have the touch. When
I was a little girl, in the birthday party pictures, I am the one
with the scowl. And the Kool-Aid stain down my dress. Scratch-
ing at my miserable stiff petticoats. Wanting bad to kick off the
patent leather shoes. Watching the gifts being opened and
thinking, Okay, when she opens mine, she'll have three Mr.
Potato Heads.

Then the whole junior high party thing that stretched for
me through college. Lots of standing around in spilled drinks and
potato chips goo. Too much Leslie Gore. Actually the most
horrible party of that era was the one my friend Priscilla and I
and ten other ruling princesses gave our senior year in high
school. We called it Midnight Madness and we told the boys they
all had to wear tuxedos and told the other girls they all had to
wear black. We wore white. Or maybe it was the other way
around. Anyway we were extremely pleased with ourselves and
it was very sophisticated and everybody had a terrible time.   I
won't even go into my own children's birthday parties. Except
to note the disaster when Darth Vader drove up in a large two-

toned Buick and everybody screamed and cried and hid in closets and under beds and one child threw up. And that was the good party.

I'm terrible at parties. So I hate to admit it but it's quite clear that Jesus just loved them. Really, Jesus was a kind of party animal. He went to them all the time. He chatted up the folks, stood around listening to the music, enjoyed the gathering. He did his first miracle at a party, turning water into wine at a wedding in Cana of Galilee so that the celebration that had already been going for two days could keep on going and going and going—which just sends shivers down my spine.

Now, if you are like me and the thought of a God who loves parties is chilling, we've got a lot in the Bible to worry about. God is a party thrower. From the first "Let there be . . ." to David dancing naked before the Ark down the streets of Jerusalem to the angels and cherubim and seraphim hollering and cutting up for the shepherds to the last supper which is the party we repeat every week. All through the ages in the waltzes of the stars and the rock and roll of the atoms and in the joy and wonder of children and of adults who remember how to be children—all through the ages, there it is, God throwing a party and wanting everybody in the dance.

Like Jesus' story about once upon a time a king gave a party. A wedding party. And nobody on the invitation list much wanted to come, and they all said, "Naaa-ahh" the first time he sent some people out to ask them. But the king in Jesus' story looked around and saw that they'd already cooked the tenderloin and made the cheese balls and lots of marinated shrimp and cunning little tarts. Really, there were all manner of things to delight the eye and the heart and he just couldn't stand for people to miss it. So he sent his folks out to ask again.

But people kind of laughed and said, Oh, we don't have time to go to this silly old wedding with you. A lot of them said, We don't have time to party; we've got to make money. And several said, We have a very important church committee meeting where we will attend to critical business so we can't party. And some said, God, I feel so overwhelmed with my family responsibilities, I can't fool around at a party. And several cliques said, We don't want to go to some party where we might run into somebody we don't know. We just want to have a private party for ourselves. And one woman said, I can't party because I am trying to find myself and a party with people would get in the way. And a guy said, I can't party, I'm very busy nursing a grudge. And so forth. Many turndowns. Many regrets.

And still the king asked over and over again. He telephoned and wrote and e-mailed, always inviting, always offering the banquet, the music, the dance. Everybody come. Good and bad, mean and gentle, old, young, lost, found, beautiful and plain, brave and chicken. Everybody come. There's this party. Don't miss the party. Come to the wedding. Come to my party.

Isaiah describes a party, too. He says picture it spread out all over a great big holy mountain, a feast of rich food, of well-aged wines. And everybody can find the place that just suits them at this party. There is a path beside some still waters where the quiet ones gather to read their books and go fishing and take naps. And the ones who love to dance have the music of the stars. And the little children can play hide and seek and someone who loves them always finds them. And the old people have rocking chairs and sunsets to watch and gentle breezes. And there are beautiful tables spread before everyone. It is the kind of banquet where nobody has to listen to a speech but everyone is heard. And everyone looks at each other and says, surely my cup runneth over.

Now this is hard for a lot of us to believe. Sometimes along the way, the church forgets why we come together, so we forget what a party with God looks like. We think maybe God wants us to stand around all through our lives in scratchy petticoats and tight shoes and ties that strangle. We forget to put on our real party clothes. Which, by the grace of God, turns out to be the grace of God. Clothing us, surrounding us, covering us. Forgiving us. Healing us. Free. Grace. For us. You and me. Take it. Free garment of grace. Choose. Take it and live. Reject it and shiver outside the party, standing naked in the cold.

And one day at the party, Isaiah says, our King will do a miracle. He will destroy on this mountain the shroud that is cast over all peoples, the sheet that is spread over all nations. In the middle of the party, in the giving and receiving, in the loving and the truth-telling, in the healing, in the forgiveness of sins, in the breaking of the bread and in the wine, our King will do a miracle. He will swallow up death forever. And wipe away the tears from all faces. And the disgrace of the people God will take away.

So in the best of times, in the worst of times, even in the valley of the shadow of death, we don't have to fear any evil. Because what they tell us, Jesus and Isaiah and the psalm singer and all of them, what they tell us is that we are the guests of honor at the party of the King.

Say 'Cheese'

In my family we take a lot of pictures, but sort of in spurts. Sometimes we take a lot of pictures just because we finally remember to get the film. Sometimes it's because we got another brand-new, absolutely fool-proof camera and hope springs eternal. Then we get the pictures back, and they're not very good either.

Mostly we take a lot of pictures when there is a big event or a lovely moment we want to capture, like a wedding or when a child is born. We do better at this picture taking with first children, don't we? Their earliest smiles, their first steps, wobbling, laughing, arms stretched out toward the one behind the camera. And then birthday parties and hats and cakes and vacations at the beach and family trips to see someplace wonderful. And we take snapshots of graduations and anniversaries and celebrations when we have somehow grabbed whatever gold ring we were after. So in my family, probably like yours, we have lots of snapshots of people smiling, saying cheese. At least I think they're smiling. Like I said, we're not real good at picture taking.

Earthly Good

And we've got stacks of these things in drawers all over the house, maybe just like you. One day, I tell myself, I'm going to have them all in perfect order. And I'm going to get rid of all the shadowy ones and the just-out-of-focus ones and the ones where we look not-so-good and the ones where it is a mystery who all is in the picture or what exactly was the occasion. I tell myself, one day I'm going to clean them all out and put just those few perfect pictures in a nice album with neatly lettered captions. And then we can sit and look at them and remember our life and count our blessings. And maybe some day, if I ever have grand-children, and then if they have grandchildren, they'll have some really good pictures of us—of who we are and what our lives have been like and what's been important for us.

Except, of course, who we are doesn't always look so good, isn't always smiling. Not me and mine. Not you and yours. None of us is always smiling. And what our lives are like is so mixed up in the lovely and the unlovely. Our woes and our blessings lie so close together, folding into each other, twining around each other so intimately that we cannot separate them without doing violence to the truth. So maybe beside the wedding pictures, you need the close-to-divorce pictures, the pictures when you hurt each other and then choose to forgive, however clumsily. Or you grow away from each other and, here's an ungraceful pose, you lurch back together, because what else is there? Or next to the wedding picture, maybe there does need to be a divorce picture because the marriage did die and that was the bitter truth and you had the unlovely guts to admit it.

Or beside the picture of your little girl, holding hands with her dad, all decked out in her Easter dress, maybe you need another picture of her daddy up late some night patting her and holding her hair back while she throws up. Because that's when she knew he really loved her. Or next to the picture of your kids smiling at each other on cue for the camera, you need a picture of them screaming at each other because they did a lot of that. And everybody lived through it. And, by the grace of God, you're still a family.

Or beside the picture of you and your friends on vacation together you need the picture of you and your friends staring at each other in disappointment because you've hurt each other's feelings or you discover your values are shockingly different. But you hang in because, well, by the grace of God, you're friends.

Or next to the picture of you and your colleagues at work, winning some award or something, looking happy and busy and fulfilled, you need a picture of you and your colleagues bored out of your minds with each other and with the job or sniping at each other under pressure. And then going back to work together the next day, because, hey, you need the money and because you're a grumpy team but a team nevertheless.

And for church, right next to the pictures of our congregations laughing or praying or singing carols, we need some pictures of us angling for a pew on Easter. Or arguing over the way we spend money. Or sitting in a meeting and enduring somebody, maybe me, who's droning on and on.

Or, to tell the truth of who we are, we need some pictures of us at a funeral. To tell the truth of us, we'd have to have some pictures of us weeping, because we have to say goodbye to somebody we love. We have to have some snapshots of us heartbroken. Needing each other and God, bad.

Earthly Good

Heart broken. Heart open. There's the woe and the blessing for people like us who follow a God on a cross, which is, of course, our clearest, most focused snapshot of God. On a cross. And God doesn't look so great. Pretty unsuccessful. Pretty pitiful. Heartbroken. Ungodlike. Not much of a savior. And remember, not even on a golden cross like what is in church. Not a golden cross between two candlesticks, but a cross between two thieves on the town garbage dump. If we want a picture of God, well, that's what we're stuck with. If we want a more successful god, a more dignified god, I'm afraid we'll just have to try some god other than the one revealed in Jesus Christ.

To be honest, I used to think Jesus didn't like people like me. I used to think that, with enough money and education and self-sufficiency, I kind of got on his nerves. In the gospels, he seems irritated with rich people so often, usually because they won't give enough to others. You remember the stories. The rich young ruler who sadly turns away from Jesus because he didn't want to give. The rich fool who builds the barns to hoard his harvest and dies that very night. Or the rich guy who stuffs himself at lunch every day, never noticing the beggar Lazarus at his gates, and then is cast into outer darkness forever. Those are just a few of the snapshots of rich people in the gospel of Luke. So I have thought that maybe Jesus just didn't like my kind, which includes, compared to the rest of the world, all middle class Americans. But now I know different. Because I have been around long enough to know in the depths of my being that God loves us very much. I just think Jesus worries about us a lot. I don't think he's mad. I just think he says, woe is them, with a worried look. I think he is scared for us. I think he is scared that, clutching our possessions, our accomplishments, we'll miss the boat, miss the party, miss the meal, miss the life.

Because it's hard to see God, find God, know God, love God when we get busy posing like the strongest, richest, happiest people that ever walked. Because it's just terribly hard to connect with God when we don't think we need God. It's just a terrible curse to suffer from the awful soul-killing delusion of self-sufficiency.

All of us know the word 'woe' from the inside. The woes are part of the truth of what it means to be human. Yen and yang, blessing and curse, heartbreak and heart open, life and death. We know that. And yet and still we people with much riches, much laughter, much power, we say 'cheese' so well. We, more than poor people, can delude ourselves. So, for Christ's sake, remember that self-sufficiency is not the truth of us, lest we forget our need for the One who made us and gives us every breath.

In the church's way of marking time, the season of epiphany is the season of glimpses of the Holy. The season of snapshots of God. Take it from Jesus. For your epiphanies, look in the shadows. Look in your griefs, your needs, your hungers, your heartbreak. Look in the places where you are broken open. And say your prayers.

Then, look at your neighbors—the ones not smiling, the ones out of focus, the ones that we know way down deep that there, but for the luck of the draw, go us. Look at your neighbors, your poor neighbors especially, and work at figuring ways to 'respect

Earthly Good

the dignity of every human being' like we said we would when we were baptized.

Then maybe, if we truly try to see ourselves and truly try to see our neighbors, we will have the grace truly to see God. Which is to say, maybe we will have the grace to see the cross, see through the cross. Where the woes and the blessings of the universe meet and point to the mystery of God. The ground is level there at the cross, where we—rich and poor—can find our place, our truest image, our heart. So picture yourself with the rest of God's children. At the foot of the cross. Where you will find your life.

Holy New Light

Last December my husband and I went to the planetarium out at the local high school to see the program they'd put together about the Christmas Star. We were part of a very small crowd. There was a young couple and their little baby. I'm kind of suspicious of little babies at the movies and so forth, and this one did look like a potential troublemaker.

There was an older man there who turned out to have worked on the renovation of the planetarium. He was proud of the job that the volunteers had done and rightfully so, it looked state of the art. He also turned out to be the grandfather of the little baby and proud of her too. As far as I was concerned, the jury was still out on the baby.

We chatted while the clock moved on a little past the hour when we were supposed to get started. If I get somewhere on time (which is kind of rare) I am like a reformed smoker—very haughty about anybody who is late. Plus, the baby situation was tenuous. She was goo-gooing now, but we all know how quickly goo-gooing can turn on you.

We looked at the director with that sort of smiling, questioning look that you try first when somebody isn't doing what they are supposed to be doing. And he said that he was waiting just a minute since he'd hate for somebody to come in the middle.

The baby situation was definitely ominous. She cranked up a little whine. And then, lo and behold, in the door slouched maybe ten teenage boys. At least ten. With the baggy pants and the tennis shoes bigger than Rhode Island and t-shirts with ornery slogans on them. I'm thinking, oh great, a reform school class outing. Okay, maybe a scout troop, but I didn't think so.

They sat down, way down, sliding low into the seats, spreading out all over the planetarium, which is in the round. Two or three were very near us, looking sullen, as if this Christmas star thing sure wasn't their idea, as if they were dragged there, which they probably were. The baby took it all in, deciding whether to really tune up.

There we were—fifteen people and a baby—and I'm thinking, this isn't looking very promising. Scruffy looking kids, a nice older man who seemed a wise kind of guy but after all a stranger, and the young couple all wrapped up in their baby. The baby, of course, who was totally unpredictable. This was not the crowd I would have picked to catch the Christmas spirit with. Not by a long shot.

Then the lights began to dim and dim all the way to pitch-black dark. And for a moment there, in that deep velvet dark, it is as if I was totally alone. Nobody else in the world—not the dear one next to me or the sullen kid four seats over, much less the strangers scattered all around the room. For a moment I dwelt in a land of deep darkness, in a round, dark world all alone. And as it stretched on, the time of darkness closed in on me and I was strangely afraid.

And then slow, slow, slow above and all around the stars began to glimmer. And the planets began to glow just barely red or yellow or green, just a glow. And very distant suns beamed, the hottest ones blue like burning ice. And, my word, the heavens enveloped us, moving in some kind of stately circle dance all over and around us. Truly the stars reveal God's glory. All around our little world, the faces—somehow transformed—were turning toward the light. Even the sullen boy four seats over had his head thrown back in wonder and delight, a small smile flickering. And the little baby went "ooohh." For all of us.

The show was great. Good science. Good theology. Very interesting. But the best moment for me came in seeing our little motley crew afresh, lost in joy and wonder.

There was another motley crew so long, long ago. A very unlikely crowd, not at all whom you'd pick to catch the Christmas spirit with. Smelly shepherds, baffled wise men, a first-time father scared out of his wits and a young woman just done with birthing, worn out, exhausted, hurting, And of course the baby. Who, as you know, turned out to be a real troublemaker, One who does, in truth, turn the world upside down. Who turns these words inside out—Wonderful counselor, Almighty God, Everlasting Father, Prince of Peace. Come as a little child for them so long ago and for us, so that through him, any old motley crew can start out—even in the dark—and end up seeing each other and ourselves in a holy new light. Through the eyes of that little

73

baby, any old motley crew can see that we are beloved beyond the telling in the light of the gaze of God who comes to us again, this dark and starless night.

O little town of Bethlehem,
How still we see thee lie;
Above thy deep and dreamless sleep the silent stars go by;
Yet in thy dark streets shineth the Everlasting Light.
The hopes and fears of all the years are met in thee tonight.

Flocks and Outsiders

Late one afternoon, I walked out to feed the birds. Of course the birds around my house only like very expensive bird-seed. So I'd mixed up the cut corn and the thistle and the shiny black sunflower seed and the striped and there I went out to the feeder with a meal that probably costs more than what my husband and I would cook for ourselves that evening. As usual, everybody scatters, including Templeton, our field rat, who just thinks he's a bird. Everybody flees from the intruder—except . . . Except. This is odd. I walk slowly, slowly, closer. I'm five feet away. A bird stays on the feeder. Well, isn't he a weirdo, I think. I stand for a while and move closer. I'm three feet, two feet away, one foot. And there is still this tiny bird on the feeder. Frizzled looking, frumpled feathers every which away, so maybe very young. Quietly, I say, buddy, how are you? And he keeps eating and eating, ravenous. After a while I reach, slowly, slowly, reach, reach, touch him, and he keeps eating. I hold seed out to him. He pecks. I stroke his back; smooth, soft, and underneath the bony structure, the heart beating, beating. I am awe struck.

He turns toward me. And now I see his head. Malformed. One eye socket crusted, grotesquely swollen way out of proportion and shut, perhaps the eyeball not there. The other eye, though, sees finally and suddenly he is scared unto death. He flaps, flops, beats the air. I did not realize how hard it is to fly. He flop-flaps, looping his way over to the roof of the house and crash-lands. Wobbles, looking around there with the one eye for maybe five seconds. Then, he tucks his head under his wing and passes out, terrified, I guess, from his encounter with the alien, exhausted and alone.

He is alone, of course, because he is sick. And for the next few days I watch him—he's hard to miss with the loopy flight and the swollen head—and the unfolding drama that began five minutes after the gates of paradise clanged shut. The other birds want him gone. They peck him in the head and drive him away from the food, away from the safety of the flock because in the mystery of creation, that's how the group gets stronger and stronger. The weak and the different are shunned and die off. The fit and strong survive to breed ever-stronger progeny. And the species improves. And as for the deformed baby bird or kitten or baboon, or even worse, as for the alien—well, it's too bad for them but that's the wisdom of Mother Nature. The strong get stronger. Which is Good. The weak and wounded die off. Which is Necessary. And the herd always closes ranks against the alien. That's the God-given order of things. And that's just the way it is, if you are an animal.

But what about us? Oh, I think every strand of DNA in our bodies remembers the laws of Mother Nature. We are wired just like the birds and the tigers: it's dangerous to be weak; and it's dangerous to be the stranger.

76

So no wonder you walk into a new classroom the first day of school and feel afraid. I have a friend who walked into second grade, took one look around and said, I think I'd better go back to the first grade. What if you aren't smart enough to do the work? Or what if the flocks are formed and you don't fit in?

Or you walk into a new church. What if you look lost, do the wrong thing—all this getting up and getting down and finding your way in this crazy prayer book. What if no one speaks to you? Or, for the introverts among us, horrors, what if someone does speak to you?

It's just hard to be a stranger—in a new town or new job or new marriage or whatever. I remember as a young bride looking at my husband's family and being afraid. Who were all these people and how would I fit in? And why do they give Christmas presents on Christmas Eve instead of Christmas morning like everybody knows you are 'sposed to? It's just hard to join a flock. And it's hard to let somebody in your flock.   Once you get in, it's hard not to want the circle to close behind you as if there might not be enough belonging to go around. It feels good in the flock and it's hard to be an outsider.

And, oh, it's hard to be weak. To be vulnerable. To get older and need some help with things you used to do for your-self. That's embarrassing. Or to get sick. People have told me that they feel ashamed of getting seriously ill, that sickness is humiliating. Or to have trouble in your family or on the job or whatever. It's hard to feel vulnerable like that. You don't want anybody to know because, because . . . . Well—if we traced those feelings back and back—what if the flock shuns you? What if the herd nudges you out and you are left there, weak and alone?

Now if animal is all there is to us, then being a stranger, being weak, being old, being sick, being different in any way from the strongest members of the herd is bad. So a gay teen-ager contemplates suicide—which by the way is an epidemic situation in this country—because the pain of hiding and the danger of ostracism is just excruciating. Or a sick person turns their face to the wall—why bother. I'm not worth anything to anybody anymore. Or an old couple gets isolated because they're afraid of what will happen if someone sees the mess things have come to. Or somebody quits coming to church because they've gotten a divorce and they feel like a failure. As if church is mainly for the maintenance of the herd, for the strong and sure and the rest of us better hide our isolation, our pain, our fear. As if Christians should be ashamed of needing God and each other.

Sometimes we forget, don't we, that the sign of our faith is a cross—a sign of alienation and weakness and death . . . and resurrection. Sometimes we forget that our journey of faith is to move out of the herd and trust the power of God, power, as Paul says, made perfect in weakness.

Even Jesus had to learn to move out of the herd. Even he had to learn in his bones what God told Isaiah to declare to the people, *My house shall be called a house of prayer for all peoples,* even—maybe especially—the outcast and the sick and the wounded, even—even maybe especially—the stranger. Even Jesus had to learn that.

And he learned the breadth of God's love the way we all do. From someone outside our herd. A stranger. An outcast. Jesus thought he was called only to his tribe, until the Canaanite woman, weak and impure, cried out in her desperation for her sick daughter and called Jesus, through the grace of God, into a wider belonging, a more universal ministry. Even Jesus had to grow, had to open his arms wider than he wanted, had to learn from the stranger, how very wide God's mercy is.

And then, when the time was fulfilled, he was ready. To stretch out his arms upon the cross, to offer himself, in the perfect power of weakness, a gift—not for his little herd, but for the whole world.

There's a wideness in God's mercy like the wideness of the sea.
There is kindness in his justice that is more than liberty.
There is welcome for the sinner and more graces for the good;
There is mercy with the Savior; there is healing in his blood.

Earthly Good

V Door Openers

Our daughter will be a first-year teacher next fall. She's loved school from the first day of kindergarten with the beautiful Miss Borgshulte on into first grade with the sainted Miss Cooper, who taught both of our children. If I could have figured out a way to be in Miss Cooper's class and sit in her lap, and have her read me stories, and laugh her deep, honeyed kind of bellowing laugh, well I would have gone to first grade, too.

Anna walked to school every day, just one street over from us, as fast as her chubby little legs would carry her. Unfortunately, once she got there she talked so much that it was touch-and-go for a while as to whether she would ever settle down and learn her state capitols or how to write a paragraph or how many planets circle the sun. She just loved being at school with her friends and, as we say in Tennessee, "visiting."

In the fifth grade—the powers-that-be having noticed her skills in chatting—she was given the job of her dreams. She was named one of several "car door openers." Every morning she and her colleagues would wait in front of the school. As the cars with little kids rolled up, the car-door-opener team would spring into action and, of course, open the car doors and say hey, how are you? and help the little children tumble out safely.

Then they would watch over them as they staggered up the steps with their Snoopy lunch boxes and their coats and mittens all askew, ready for a big day in kindergarten or first or second grade. What a joy to be a door opener for others who were walking into a new world, a larger world full of surprises and possibilities and other doors.

Every year, we honor the high school graduates in our congregation. I think about these wonderful young people and about all of the teachers and scout leaders and sports league coaches and camp counselors and church school leaders and all the gentle armies of neighbors and friends who have been life-giving for them down through the years. Not because they had all the answers but because they were willing to take the time to be door openers for others.

Do you wonder sometimes if you know enough to be a faithful, life-giving person? Do you know the doctrines and the rules well enough to be a good Christian or Jew or Muslim or Buddhist or whatever holy faith through which you understand our Creator?

I don't think I know enough, and I've been to a fancy seminary. But then I remember the people who have taught me the meaning of the words of my faith: trust, mercy, endurance, courage, repentance, forgiveness, joy, and, over all and in all, love. They didn't throw a catechism at me or beat me over the head with a Bible or any other book. They just lived these words:

Trust. Mercy. Endurance. Courage. Repentance. Forgiveness. Joy. Love. And doors opened in my soul.

You know the door openers in your life. What about calling one or writing one a letter? I am sure most of them have no idea how much they have mattered to you.

Earthly Good

Prisons

Christians have long made a habit of landing in jail. One of the more bizarre accounts in the book of Acts is of a slave-girl who had been making her owners plenty of money by yelling out people's fortunes until she became entranced by Paul's teaching. She began following Paul and Silas around and yelling out the truth—that Paul and Silas were servants of God and knew the door to salvation. But she yelled that with no understanding, no grasp of the possibilities of freedom for herself. She just kept yelling about salvation in a kind of inane way—like we sometimes still do in the church.

Well, this yelling with no understanding just got on Paul's last nerve. He didn't want an ad campaign about the faith; instead he wanted believers in the faith, who would, through their faith, spread the good news. So he prayed to God to cure her of her demonic mouthing of that which she did not compre-hend. And in that very hour she came to her senses, free at last of the inane hollering.

Her owners were furious because she wouldn't do her circus trick anymore and they would lose the income. They accused

Paul and Silas of disturbing the peace, because the owners were very, very sensitive about the peace of their pocketbook.

The city fathers, who were also keenly sensitive folks, being especially sensitive about the issues surrounding upset rich people, heard their complaint. And in order to keep the peace of the rich people, the city fathers beat Paul and Silas half to death and threw them in jail, telling the jailer to make sure they stay jailed or else. So the jailer got the message that his freedom depended on their bondage. He got the message—as old as Cain and Abel—that my good standing depends on my standing on your neck—and he put them in the deepest, darkest, most closed up, innermost cell of all.

And then the weird thing happens. The Holy Spirit thing. In the depths of the prison, weighed down by chains, the prisoners offer up their prayers, lift up their hearts. Not mouthing religious platitudes but speaking the words that are their way and their truth and their life. And, my God, it happens. The Holy Spirit thing. And the world turns inside out. And the roles flip upside down. And the captive is free. And the captor knows his bondage. And they rejoice and break bread together, so communion emerges in the strange mystery of the freedom of the jail. And the freedom of God shakes the foundations and sweeps through the people and the place and turns dungeon into chapel so that there is no need to escape and no desire to incarcerate.

That upside down, inside out freedom is still our way and our truth and our life. First we know the freedom in Jesus— when you read about his arrest and trial, it is so clear that he is free even on the cross, even unto death, that no one takes his life. He offers himself; he gives his life in freedom. And then we know the freedom in Paul, writing in profound freedom from prisons all across the Mediterranean, an ambassador in chains. Teaching and preaching in a voice ringing with power: "For freedom Christ has made us free," he writes wreathed in iron. And we know the words are true.

I think of other voices from prison that have touched my heart. Dietrich Bonhoeffer chose to go back into Nazi Germany because he realized he couldn't be free in England while his homeland was writhing in fear and chaos. Grace doesn't come that cheap, he said. And so he returned to the nightmare and stood against Hitler and the collaborating Christian churches and wrote to us from prison words that will free you to this day. The Nazis executed him. But really they didn't.

And Martin Luther King, Jr. writing the gospel afresh from a Birmingham jail and filling hearts with courage, and sometimes even more important, filling hearts with shame. Because, as King wrote, it wasn't the evil of the few keeping out the king-dom of God; it was the indifference of good church people. Years later, long after King's death, I read his words, and I was ashamed and I repented and found new life. An assassin's bullet cut him down. But really it didn't.

I remember another voice from prison. Not famous, this time. Really kind of a squeaky voice come to the big city from Alabama. Bob belonged to my parish in Atlanta, well entrenched when I got there. He never met a stranger and he was in the banking business and, between the two—being truly a warm, friendly guy and having a lot of people owe him money—he knew a lot of people. At church, he sang in the choir until he and the choirmaster got cross with each other. Bob could be pretty ornery about music. Bob also team-taught the three-year-olds in Sunday school, but he was absolutely never ornery with them.

In the late eighties Bob was diagnosed as HIV positive. This was before there was much management of the disease and it became a virtual prison for him. He had to retire from work in his thirties. His feet developed terrible neuropathy so that every step was agony. He went blind although he wouldn't admit it. He had a huge lesion on his nose and he was pretty hideous to look at. The disease imprisoned him as surely as iron bars. And yet, he told me, I am freer than I have ever been in my life.

So he couldn't see. And yet he saw the heights and depths and beauty and agony of being alive.

So he couldn't get around much. But on Wednesday after-noons he was the parish volunteer receptionist and he and his nurse Maureen would show up with oxygen and IV bags. He was pleased as punch when people would call in and—since he couldn't see to tell one extension from another—he would just connect folks to whomever he and God decided they needed to talk to. We all made new friends on Wednesday afternoons.

So he looked horrible. Three year olds don't care. They just loved him as he loved them. They sat around him in a gentle crooked little circle, as if they somehow knew he was fragile, and listened to that squeaky voice tell the Bible stories. And no matter what the story, they learned profound truths about courage and unconditional love.

As Bob grew weaker and moved on toward the end, he told us in no uncertain terms that we all better show up at his funeral because he wanted his mama to see us. The two of them had been having a terrible time. She came to town periodically, armed with a Bible and sixty years of hellfire and damnation hollered into her soul. She would stand over his bed and serve up platitudes about Jesus and salvation and then holler about how Bob was going straight to hell. All she could see was that Bob was gay and that was hateful beyond murder to her church and humiliating in front of her church friends. It was one of the most pathetic and demonic pastoral situations that I have ever experienced. You know the prison turning into church works both ways: a church with enough hate in it can be a terrible prison, even barring a mother from her son.

Well, we showed up all right. The church was packed. Bankers from around town in gray suits. Mamas and daddies of little ones and his Sunday school teacher friends. Members of the Bach Society, where he sang. Folks from the United Way, where he volunteered. Nurses and doctors moved by his courage. And friends from everywhere—straight and gay, old and young, poor and rich—all there, all one in Christ who prayed over and over for us to be one.

And now Bob is dead and gone all these years. But really he isn't.

Christians have long made a habit of landing in jail, even unto death. And yet. And yet. Oh grave where is thy victory, oh death where is thy sting?

Learning to Haggle

Ask, and it will be given you; search, and you will find; knock, and the door will be opened for you.
   Luke 11:9

For lots of us, there is something embarrassing about asking. Perhaps the embarrassment is left over from being a kid and not wanting to draw attention to yourself and your needs. Needing anything just seems sort of impolite. So you sit in the first grade afraid to whisper to the teacher that you would like to go to the restroom. Or you are at your new friend's house and her mother says, What would you like to drink? And you say, Oh, I don't care. And she hands you root beer, which you despise. And there you are stuck, smiling a little smile and saying thank you in a small voice while she waits for you to take a sip.

For lots of us, it just seems tacky and even dangerous to ask because once you put your need or desire out there, the ask-ee then has the power over you to say no. So we hope those around us are mind readers. Spouses, friends, everybody is supposed to read minds. And I get mad when you don't. And you get mad when I don't.

Or we slog on overburdened because we won't ask for help. Or we won't come out and tell each other what we want. Even little things.

A few weeks ago in a junk store, I saw an old, beat-up, wonderful painted pine table that I just loved. It didn't have a price on it and was being used to display other stuff so I didn't even know if it was for sale. I got up my nerve to ask the owner if she would sell it. She very nicely said, Well, I love it. But I might. I thought well, that was a good set up for a big old price, but I said, Oh good. There was a long pause. I just did not know where to go from there. So finally I asked what we did next and she said, Well, I'll name a price and then you have to haggle.

I said that I didn't know how to haggle. She said, Come on, try. You can do it. I said okay. So she named a price. I came back ten dollars lower. She sighed and said in that kind tone you use with clumsy children learning to tie their shoes, Well, that was all right, but you're s'posed to start lower.

Needless to say, my parish vestry and I agree that I should not take the lead in any financial negotiations.

Not so Abraham who was God's friend. Abraham haggled, even with God. Because he trusted God enough to be vulnerable, to ask. Even to ask God to change God's mind. Even to ask God to forgive a city gone wild. A city which had forgotten the meaning of hospitality, a city infamous for its viciousness, where predators ruled and the stranger was assaulted. Abraham—because he loved his nephew Lot—asked God to spare the city. So he questions: Will you indeed sweep away the righteous with the wicked? Far be it from you to do such a thing. What if there were fifty righteous in it? God thinks it through. Well, okay for fifty. Abraham sees the tide turning, but he is not sure he can find fifty faithful people—this is a real bad town. What about forty-five? Suppose we can't find that last five righteous people. Will you destroy the whole city for lack of five? Note how he flipped it over. Now that was good haggling. God says oh, all right. We can make do with forty-five.

And eventually, Abraham beats the Almighty down all the way to ten faithful people. Ten people who are in right relationship with God, which is what righteous means. And ten, by the way, is the number it takes to make a synagogue. To form church. So for the sake of a little church, God will spare the city. Because Abraham asks.

Asking is all through the prayer that Jesus teaches us. We ask that the reign of God come when all shall be well. We ask that we have what we need for that day, maybe so every day we will remember where all of what we have comes from. And we ask for forgiveness of sin. And we bargain that we will forgive others. And we plead that God will not lead us into testing, into the time of trial because, really, who wants to go there. Even Jesus asked that the cup be passed.

Yet it wasn't. As you remember. The cup of testing, of suffering was not passed. So even Jesus asking did not lead to an automatic yes. When you ask, the answer may be yes or it may be no or it may be wait, but somehow in faithfully asking the One who loves us simply because we are God's children, somehow in asking, the door is opened to grace.

So you ask. You even haggle. And maybe you get just what you want, just how you want, just when you want. That's what we are all hoping for isn't it? But maybe you ask for something and instead, the gift God gives is the gift of strength to endure what is, the gift of wisdom to cope, the gift of hope to look beyond the crisis or even the chronic. Perhaps instead of getting the situation changed, we are given the gift of a changed self instead. We are given more depth, more power, new life.

So you pray and God answers. Sometimes you ask, and you receive a new situation. And sometimes you ask and you receive a new you. Either way there will be new life.

Ask, and it will be given you; search, and you will find; knock, and the door will be opened. For you.

Simple Gifts

Turning

When true simplicity is gained
To bow and to bend we shan't be ashamed
To turn, turn will be our delight
'Til by turning, turning, we come 'round right.

They say, the scientists, that the primal move is turning. The universe, in the moment when all moments began, when time and space emerged from the deep heart of God, the universe, twisting in birth, exploded out – not into the form of a perfect circle or a square or a triangle or hexagon – but the universe was birthed in turning. Spiraling really, which is a lovely and complex and grace-filled kind of turning, isn't it?

And so now we watch the Milky Way spiraling across the night sky. Or we pick up a seashell and hold it to our ears and, listening deep into its swirl, we hear the sea, our mother. Or we watch the weather on TV and we see the storm coming, spiraling across the water or the land in great beauty and terrible power, and we shudder in fear for those in its path. Or maybe we look at the hands of a little baby, before the fingers get calloused or worn down or scarred and we see in her tiny whorls, the spirals of the stars and the shell and the storm and the rose. The turning, turning of all of life in the hands of a little baby.

I believe that somehow 'turning, turning 'til we come 'round right' is the movement of the Christian faith and the movement of our life together. We know that turning and spiraling in our love for each other. At our best, we do not try to make circles or squares or triangles out of each other or out of our life together. At our best we give each other room to turn, and we pray that our lives in Christ will be a centered in peace like the eye of the storm or the heart of the rose, no matter where we turn.

I believe that 'turning, turning 'til we come 'round right' is what happens in us in the moments when we connect in the deep heart of God—the same God who set the sun and moon and the stars and this fragile earth, our island home, turning — the same God that set all the heavens dancing, moving together in harmony and grace. I believe that very same God calls to us and when we turn toward God there is conversion, also known as repentance. *Metanoia*. Transformation. The old is turned new. The barren turns fruitful. The dead turns to new life. And even if only for a moment we turn, we dance, in harmony with the creation and the One who made it all.

Smudged by Grace

The first act of the Lenten season is when we gather on Ash Wednesday to say our prayers and to ask for God's forgiveness. We kneel to hear that we are dust and to dust we shall return and to receive the sign of the cross imprinted in ashes on our foreheads.

Every year the ashen smudges get me. Ashes on the baffled faces of the little children whose mothers always make them clean up for church and ashes on the foreheads of the rest of us—the worried ones and the smiling ones and the bored and the overwhelmed and the rich and the angry and the timid and the very sick and the very beautiful. Ashes on the upturned faces of all of us. So that we are smudged, every one of us—smudged with only God knows what—greed and lust and carelessness and pride and remorse and, well, every smudge of living there is.

We meet together each Ash Wednesday and we claim on that day all the ashes of our lives: all the residue of what is burned up or burned out by our sin and our weakness and our dying and our regret and our yearning for people to love us most and for God to love us best. We meet to admit all those ashes and to get smudged by grace.

I think of another meeting in the ashes—one that I saw out my office window in Atlanta on the odd day now and then. A gathering every late afternoon outside the church while people wait for the guy with the key to get there and open the door and start the AA meeting. They stand around in a lopsided circle in the garden, low voices murmuring, smoke drifting around the circle. Soft laughter. There's no smoking in the building so most everybody times it for a few more drags before the hour of abstinence.

Around Ash Wednesday, in the late winter twilight, the cigarettes are easier to see than the faces of the people, so what you see are red glows here and there. Ashes lengthening. Fingers flicking, ashes falling occasionally on somebody's shoes. S'cuse me. S'allright. The guy with the key comes. They begin to move toward the door dropping the butts and stepping, grinding, stubbing out the butt ends. Most everybody shuffles on in the door, through the ashes into the light and the heat and the meeting. But some evenings there's a hold out. Somebody hangs back. Maybe a first-timer but more likely a lots-of-timer crawling back on the wagon, because, after all, there is only one first fall per person and then lots of other falls. So, more likely, the hold-out has been to the meeting before and is shamed unto death to take the first step back.

Instead, she lights another cigarette, sits on the wall, head down, hunched over and inward. The smoke floats. The ashes settle on the concrete. And there, huddled over the ashes, I guess she decides. I guess she chooses whether to hang on alone or to risk it, turning toward the light and the heat and the meeting. To take the first step back, move through the ashes and go in with the others one more time.

The first act of the Lenten season is Ash Wednesday. Which can, of course, be any day any season. It is simply the day you choose. It is the day you choose one more time not to hang on alone but to move through the ashes toward the light and the meeting. It is the day you choose to get smudged by grace.

Finding Fault

"What does the Lord require of you but to do justice, and to love kindness, and to walk humbly with your God?"   Micah 6:8

     I was in the local county Domestic Court on Thursday. I take my turn there about once a month as part of an ongoing presence from our area Ecumenical Council. When I am there I mainly just pray. There is so much pain and anger in the room that I don't know how to be helpful, but surely saying my prayers can't hurt.

     Just the order of the thing is chaotic. Trials get reset time and time again. Victims don't show up and it's hard to know whether it's because they don't want to prosecute or they're scared to. Maybe the accused shows up, but at the arraignment he had said he didn't want a lawyer, and this time he says he does so the trial gets reset. This week one of the accused was Hispanic and the interpreter didn't show—so, reset. People sit in little clumps scattered around the room—the space has wooden pews that remind you of a church—and after a while it becomes apparent which clumps are furious with which other ones.   It is a difficult place to gather a lot of hope for the human condition and I admire the people who do their jobs there with integrity.

Thursday morning, the head public defender approached the judge with some papers and said, Your honor, I hate to bring this up, but Mrs. Smith called me and she said she was just kind of wondering why she was still in jail after you said you'd let her out. And I checked around and it looks like you put the wrong case number on the discharge papers. And the judge looked at the paper and looked at the lawyer and frowned fiercely and said, Well, now let me tell you that I am just mightily sick and tired of having my mistakes brought to my attention.

I love that. I know what he means. But then it made me wonder if the Judge of All There Is might also get mightily tired of us always bringing all of the Judge's mistakes—ourselves and each other—to the Judge's attention. So many of us are hardwired to see fault in ourselves and each other that we forget that, as Paul says, God chooses what is foolish in the world to shame the so-called wise. God chooses what is weak in the world to shame the so-called strong. So that we might not boast of our own power in the presence of God who gives us every gift, every power. So that we might walk humbly and instead of boasting about our own prowess, we might boast with peace and joy and laughter of the power of God.

Somebody said to me lately that he had become aware of how often he began prayer with 'I'm sorry.' Sometimes, he said, I can't even think of what I'm sorry for, but I'm just sorry. And I thought, what about beginning a prayer with 'thank you.' Thank you for making me and all these other people. Thank you for gifts you've given me, for the strengths. Thank you for a heart to love and hands to help and resources to give. Instead of saying thank you, how often we draw God's attention to faults and mistakes and failures, which, when you come to think of it— since we all belong to God —are basically God's design flaws. Basically, we are often bringing God's mistakes to God's attention.

Fault-finding is not walking humbly with our God. Fault-finding in ourselves or in others doesn't do much to help us do justice and love mercy. Instead we just stay self-focused. That being said, the self-recognition of spiritual needs and hungers is a gift from God and as Jesus says, blessed are we when we hunger for more righteous lives. When we long for the purity of heart that will refresh. When we mourn for love that is lost. Blessed are we when we know how unendingly our bodies and minds and spirits need God.

Really, all our fault-finding is like watching a drunk try to walk a straight line. The guy struggles so hard to concentrate and is so intent on doing it right. But he's staring down at the ground just right in front of him, and consequently there's no vision, no balance, no perspective, no grace. If only he, if only we would lift up our eyes and look for the Judge who turns out to be our Guide.

We are not equipped to walk alone. This is not a design flaw. This is a gift. When we walk humbly with God, we find balance. We have perspective. We walk with grace and so we know ever better how to do justice, how to love kindness. Which is to say we know ever better how to live thankfully through the great gift of all our days.

Earthly Good

A Truth about Love

I have a little white leather-bound King James Version of the Bible which was given to me by my grandparents when I was twelve and said my catechism. My name and the date and their names are inscribed in my grandfather's blocky engineer's handwriting, as well as a verse about building a strong foundation in Jesus Christ.

The spine of the book is tattered now. The little onionskin pages are hard to separate and the beautiful seventeenth century phrasing is sometimes obscure. I work with another translation, one with cross-references to other pieces of scripture and notes about geography and culture, as well as the original Greek and Hebrew phrasings.

The Oxford Annotated Bible is where I go to learn about the sacred words. I write all over it and lug it around and use it as a Very Important Tool. That little white King James Bible, on the other hand, is a sacred gift from people who loved me. From them I learned that the most sacred word of all is Love and that Love is most holy when it becomes flesh.

My first memory of praying with others (beyond the quick meal blessing) is of us at my grandparent's dining room table before breakfast. I would like to say that my memory is of appreciation for the breadth and beauty of my grandfather's morning prayers. But, mainly, I remember wondering if the biscuits would be cold before we finished praying for all the leaders of the known world. Those habits must have taken deep hold in my soul, however, since I spend so much of my time at prayer with my parish family.

My grandparents were very traditional, very conservative Presbyterians. One of their children followed the faith tradition of his parents; the other three did not.   If you asked our family to tell you what different verses of scripture mean, you would come up with as many different answers as there are aunts and uncles and cousins. But this is the gift that my grandparents gave to all of us: they lived the truth that the most sacred word of all is Love. No matter how we read the words in the Book, no differences in understandings of words are going to separate us. For we are bound by the Word who is Love.

So differences in how people read the Bible don't upset me. I grew up knowing that people who loved each other and me read scripture very, very differently. And that love trumped their different opinions every time. Actually, the way I read scripture is that Jesus got pretty annoyed by folks spending too much time on scriptural opinions and too little time loving their neighbors—no matter what their faiths—and thanking God for just being alive.

My grandfather was a Gideon who spent his life gently offering people Bibles to read. But then there's my Roman

Catholic husband and children whose faiths are fed primarily by the sacraments. And my Uncle Kenneth and my cousins Brooks and Isaac, who are Jews. And there's my adopted cousin Katie from China whose birth parents are Buddhists and whose Christian mother means for the child to know about her birth heritage. And there's my brother who hasn't set foot in a church in twenty years, except for my ordinations and my father's funeral, and yet he works harder to care for others than anybody else. And my grandparents loved us all, and my hope is they still watch with Love over every one of us.

Earthly Good

Listen. Trust.

Remember the stories of two faithful men. The first, Abraham, is the archetype of the faithful human being. The father not just of the Jewish faith but also the Christian and the Islamic faiths, all of us claim him as Father Abraham. And what did he do? No mighty works. Not a one. But he did two things. Just two. First, he listened. We don't know exactly how he listened—in his dreams? Out on a hill one day? In a casual conversation with Sarah in which he hears a deeper word? We don't know where or how, but when God spoke, he listened.

After Abraham listened, he trusted. By the grace of God, he trusted God. And as a result of the trust, he left behind the known—his country and his kindred and his father's house—and he wandered toward a promise that, if not true, would be cruel and ridiculous. For he was an old man—childless with a barren wife—and he was promised the fatherhood of a great nation through whom all the families of the earth would be blessed. He trusted God and he trusted that promise and many, many years later, it came true because of his listening and because of his trust. Not because of any fine deed, any works, but because God reckoned his listening and his trust as righteousness, the blessing came true. And now, oh, how we wish that all Abraham's children—Jew and Muslim and Christian —would listen and trust and remember the promise that we are called to fulfill, to be blessings not to just our own kind but to all the families of the earth. And what would it take for us to fulfill the promise? Remember Abraham. Only two things. Listen. Trust.

Now Abraham did faith on an epic scale. He listened, he trusted, he went. Someone said the three bravest words in the Old Testament are "So Abraham went." And in his listening, trusting, leaving is the first experience of the power of God to rebirth us. Father Abraham was the first man to be born again through listening and trusting and obeying the grace and the promise of the Word of God. And surely he did faith on an epic scale.

But maybe for most of us, the second "sort-of-faithful" man, Nicodemus, is more our speed. We want to listen for God, but . . . we don't really know how or maybe we don't hear so well. Or maybe we just can't imagine being important enough, mattering enough for God to notice us, talk to us, much less promise us that we would be blessings for the world. And beyond listening, we also have trouble trusting, even trusting the people we can see, much less trusting the One who is beyond our sight. And so Nicodemus is more our speed. Maybe Nicodemus could be the patron saint of the sort-of-faithful, some of whom are in church every Sunday, doing their duty, trying to do good deeds and live a clean life, but not sensing God's presence, not trusting God's providence. Yearning for faith but not knowing how to get there. To all outward appearances faithful, but inside, not really. Not really listening, not really trusting. So just sort-of-faithful.

For instance, Nicodemus was a leader, a teacher, a pillar of the Temple, senior warden probably many times over—but living a strangely sad life, what Henri Nouwen called the "filled but unfulfilled life." He just does not hear the voice of God from on high. Instead, by the strange grace of God, he hears gossip and complaints from the church people and the neighbors about this bizarre young man—touching people and healing them and turning water into wine and, in a horrifying display of anger and power, coming into the Temple and raking the money off the tables and chasing all the animals out and disrupting what had been going on in that space for as long as people could remember. It was just outrageous and when Nicodemus hears about it, part of him is disgusted but part of him wonders, he just wonders. He listens to the gossip and complaints and he wonders.

And so Nicodemus, the sort-of-faithful man, by the grace of God, leaves his comfortable home and heads across town in the dark of the night to find this strange young man because Jesus is outrageous but something powerful is coming through him and Nicodemus wonders . . . . So he comes in the dark and he says nobody could do what you do apart from the presence of God. Tell me what is going on. And Jesus says something so odd, so counter-intuitive. He says to this faithful, prayerful, steady, good-deed doing, churchgoing man, he says —you've got to start over. You've got to be born all over again. You have to be birthed anew. You have to begin again. And Nicodemus stands there in the dark, trying to listen, trying to trust, trying to connect—a 54-year-old, overweight, solid citizen. How? How on earth, he says, could I begin again? Do you want me to crawl back into my mother's womb? How at this stage of my life do I begin again? How could I do that?

You know Jesus never does tell him. Never prescribes one experience—and we Christians need to remember that and call each other to account when somebody talks like there is only one way to get to the new life. Jesus just says well, it's like the wind blowing—you don't know where from or where to. You just breathe in the breeze and you begin again and you live afresh.

And Nicodemus still stands there. Baffled. But not turning away. Thinking to himself, like all of us do. Wondering, well, maybe I can begin again. What would we do differently if we took the chance? Because no matter how stable, how settled, we do have the chance. How would you grow up differently? Because no matter how old you are, you can still grow—and differently. How would you begin again? We know Nicodemus did, for he reappears in the story—not as a Pharisee yelling "crucify him"—but as a friend, who, with Joseph of Arimethea, brings the spices and the myrrh and the aloe to tenderly prepare Jesus for the grave. So, like Abraham, Nicodemus began again, and on Easter morning, don't you know, he found surprising, amazing new life.

Martin Buber says that "the young are those at any age who have not unlearned what it means 'to begin'." That's what Abraham did, what Nicodemus did. They listened. They trusted. They began again—new journeys—one across wilderness, one just across his own hometown, among his own people. And through them, all of earth has been blessed.

Say your prayers and listen for the wind—it may be even in idle chatter or on the TV or in a business meeting or a telephone call. Say your prayers and listen for the wind to blow—from where, who knows? Going where, who knows? You can begin again. Listen for the Wind. Trust the Windweaver.

Taking Offense at Mrs. Caldwell

When you and I were very young, just little babies, we would see a block of color—maybe an old red ball—and we would be transfixed by the wonder of red. Or we'd grab a pot and bang it on the floor and chortle for the delight of the sound. Or we'd get a spoonful of strained bananas from the baby food jar and we'd smile wide as if we were at a five star restaurant. When we were babies, we had no taste.

When we were a little older, and a friend shared a toy or the lady at the bank drive-through gave us a lollipop or a neighbor brought us comic books when we had the chicken pox, why, we were just so glad to get the gift. We never wondered if the givers were acceptable—if our friend believed the right theology as they passed you the Etch-A-Sketch or if the lollipop-giving bank teller had a hidden marketing agenda or if the comic book-bringing neighbor was too tacky to talk to. But then we grow up and get smart, don't we? And we know about ulterior motives and gifts with strings attached and advertising giveaways and gifts whose giver is, well, not our kind.

I can actually remember when—in my mind—an old friend morphed into an unacceptable person. Mrs. Caldwell, who I knew was a teacher somewhere, lived a few doors down from us and often stopped by with different treats. She taught me little songs and how to play canasta and once took a wonderful picture that I still have of me and my boon companion, a cat named Batsie Bootsie. Mrs. Caldwell had fat sausage curls all over her head, just like Aunt Pitty-Pat in *Gone with the Wind,* and on each cheek was a small, bubblegum-pink, perfectly round circle of rouge. I knew she was very beautiful because she loved me and showed it.

Well, the years go by. We moved to another neighborhood. I worked very hard throughout my career at Bailey Junior High to become cool and achieved a fragile success, but I was aware that it could collapse like a house of cards at the Taj Mahal of Coolness, Murrah High School. So in the fourth period of my first day of classes, who turns out to be my tenth grade algebra teacher? Mrs. Caldwell—complete with sausage curls and rouge circles—and she was the laughing stock of the school. She was so glad to see me. Her old friend. To protect the guilty, I will now close the curtain on that little scene.

You know, Jesus had it so right. If you want to know what is holy and what is of God, look and see what's happening. Is there love going on? Are gifts of love being given? Is there healing? Are the blind being helped to see what really matters? Is there strengthening? Are the crippled being helped to walk on their own? Is new life coming? Are the dead coming to life? Is there love going on? Are gifts of love being given? Because if there is love—no matter the creed of the giver, the circumstance of the gift or the trappings—no matter what, if love is going on, Christ is there because Love is there. And blessed be anyone who takes no offense at Love.

I think Christians have a special job to do. I think our gift and our job description is to not take offense at love; our job description is to notice and appreciate and thank God for the gifts of love wherever and through whomever we see or hear love. I really believe our gift and our job description is to not take offense. Not to take offense at people who are different, at communities of faith that are different, not to take offense at God's love which can show up in the most peculiar ways. We live in a country where the body of Christ has been splintered into many, often tiny, sometimes suspicious little groups. We religious folks take inordinate offense at each other.

We live in a world where fear of the different runs deep and where prejudice is often masked by piety. I believe the gift we can give is not to judge the judging ones, the suspicious ones— that's God's job—but to admit that we know what it feels like be prejudiced, to take offense at the different.

We've all had our Mrs. Caldwells.

Blessed are the ones who take no offense at love, who rejoice when the blind see, the lame walk, the hungry get fed, the dirty get cleaned up, the lifeless live, the poor hear great news. However awkwardly given, however peculiar the giver, blessed are we when we are just so glad to see love. That's our gift and our job description. Blessed is anyone, Jesus says, who takes no offense at me.

Earthly Good

Mathematics of the Heart

Peter asks Jesus: How many times should I forgive? As many as seven times? Jesus says to him, not seven times but I tell you seventy seven times. Or, some manuscripts say, seventy times seven.

Oh . . . . . That many times?

Do you remember your teachers telling you about the beauty in mathematics? Look at the architecture of geometry, the elaborate rhythms of trigonometry, the mystery of algebra so that if you know x, you can discover y. Notice the elegance of calculus and wonder that all of that clarity and beauty is in the service of human knowing.

All that calculation we can use to make the engines that roar and the skyscrapers that reach to the heavens and the markets that hum. We can harness all of that precision to guide the surgeon's steel plunging towards its target. Or to guide the missile. We can crank all the numbers and even predict the likely time of our death.

We can count to a trillion. We can divide the atom and measure the wobbles of the stars. So why do so many of us struggle with the mathematics of the heart? Why do we fail to find the answers to our deep word problems? Why can't we pick the multiple choices that lead to beauty and integrity?

Why can't we solve the equations in conflicted relationships or draw the geometry of a just city? Why can't we find the sines and co-sines of love, the logarithms of forgiveness? Why do we struggle so? Many of us are good at math. Why can't we multiply goodness? How do we subtract sin? Why are we so proficient at division? Which leads us back to the question at hand, how many times should we forgive?

Now that is an interesting question, an old question. Maybe for a few of us a rhetorical question, as in: just in case anybody sins against me, how often should I forgive? Seven times? Would that about do it?

But for some of us at least, maybe most of us, forgiveness is not an academic question. Most of us at some time or another have somebody in our lives who just keeps hurting us. How do you forgive the friend who just keeps taking from you? Or the boss who just keeps slapping you down? Or the acquaintance who slanders? Or the partner who breaks your heart and then does it again? Most of us have somebody who just keeps trespassing against us.

And what about when you or me or somebody we love is struck down at random? What about when somebody we love gets wounded by outrageous slings and arrows? How do we forgive God? How do we forgive the One who was supposed to watch over us?

I suspect that for most of us the question of forgiveness is not academic. We've known the gnawing in the gut, the ache of resentment, the sleepless night, the vengeful daydream. So Jesus says just do it. Forgive. Not just seven times but more-than-you-can keep-up-with times. What we want to know is how to do that.

I don't know. Forgiving is not my strong point—I can count too well. But when I think about those who know the mathematics of the heart in my life, my professors of heart mathematics, here's what I've noticed:

You who forgive freely, you have a certain lightness. You don't take every slight so seriously. And when something really is a serious trespass, one of my artists of forgiveness told me, Look, just because I decide to let go of my anger, doesn't mean the other person didn't do something bad. It just means I don't have to make it my life's work to hang on to the fury. I choose to let go and, as they say, let God.

You who forgive freely, you have a certain lightness, the lightness of letting go.

You who forgive, I think you know about being forgiven. I think you know from the other side about forgiveness of sins. In a time of great brokenness, someone said to me that he had sat in church all his life, but now he *got* it. Being there when everything is okay is fine, he said. The church was pretty, the music was great, it was good to see friends. But being in the Body of

Christ when you are wracked with guilt and somehow the voice of Jesus breaks through with 'your sins are forgiven. Get up and walk.' Now that's the power of God.

And some people exude that power because they know on the inside about being forgiven. Which means you know your insides. You who forgive know the darkness within. Carl Jung looked at Jesus' commandment to love your enemy and asked this haunting question: What if I should discover that the very enemy himself is within me? That I myself am the enemy who must be loved? What then?

You who forgive know how to forgive the enemy within.

Speaking of enemies, I think you who forgive know Ghandi's truth that bravery consists, not in killing, but in dying.

You who forgive, I think you sometimes fake it. Which seems to work. I never can think my way into a new way of acting toward somebody. I have to act my way into a new way of thinking. Do you remember the story of the hideous man who wore the beautiful mask? One day someone snatched the mask off, and my God, he had become beautiful underneath. So you who forgive, I think you sometimes fake it. And that seems to work.

Finally you who forgive, you get it. That forgiveness is not just about what happens to the other person. Not even mostly about what happens to the other person. Forgiveness is about what happens to us. Remember the prayer that Jesus taught us: Forgive us our trespasses as we forgive those who trespass against us. That is God's economy, the multiplication of grace in God's mathematics of the heart.

So back to the question: How many times should I forgive? Oh, Jesus laughs, Seventy-seven. Four hundred and ninety. Who cares? More than you can remember to keep up with. Can't do it can you? Still seething are you? Full of poison, are you? Now we're talking. That is where we begin: with you. Turn to me and I will show you, forgive you, love you how.

The Sting of Chlorine

The first house I remember is one on St. Mary's Street in a little, leafy neighborhood surrounding Belhaven College in Jackson, Mississippi. I can't remember the inside except for bookcases that my next-door neighbor and I swung from playing Robin Hood and Maid Marian. In the tiny front yard, there was a sprawling mimosa tree that floated pink feathery boas all over the driveway and had a chronic case of caterpillars, which we squashed with our '54 two-toned Ford.

Eventually I was allowed to walk one direction down the street to our elementary school. And a year or two later, oh heaven, I could walk the other way down the street to a park called Riverside. I never saw the river part, but never mind; the park had the world's largest swimming pool—a massive and glorious affair with three diving boards. Presiding over the scene on tall, white, wooden thrones were unapproachable, godlike figures with silver whistles who sparked my first vocational dream. Maybe life-guarding is still what I'm after.

You didn't just stroll willy-nilly into Riverside Pool. There was a heavy, chain-link fence all around except for the entry where you paid your dime and turned to the right for the girls or the left for the boys. Both passageways were lined with mighty showers so that whether you wanted to or not, you were pummeled with sprays and washed within an inch of your life before you set foot in the water, which was, by the way, about one part chlorine to one part H_2O. You could smell the chemicals a block off. We were big on chlorine in Mississippi. Fluoride was a communist plot, but chlorine was good and would pucker the germs and dirt right off your fingers.

At night, the huge arc lights of that swimming pool shone round with an aura of silver rays pointing out into the darkness, almost to the stars. It was a vision, the Riverside swimming pool, and I loved it with that fierce love you have for childhood shrines.

Of course, what I didn't let myself realize was that the lights didn't beckon every child. In those days before air-conditioning, from the first hot flush of early Mississippi June through the sweaty blanket of August, the lights shone only to welcome very pale children. If your skin was creamy coffee or mocha or dark chocolate, well, you couldn't come near the cool waters unless you were a white child's nursemaid and then you sat behind the fence and fanned your steaming face. Because dark skin, was, oh my, too much even for chlorine. Looking back, it was as if only bleached people were allowed. When integration came, the horrified city fathers drained the pool, locked the gates and turned off the lights. The city eventually bulldozed the remains—a monument of ruins dedicated to a mean sort of purity and a cut-off-your-nose-to-spite-your-face sort of community vision.

There is an Hasidic tale in which the old master asks his students how they know when the darkness is leaving and the dawn is coming. One says that it is when we see a tree in the distance and know that it is an oak and not a juniper. Another says when we can see an animal and know that it is a fox and not a wolf. No, says the teacher. We know the darkness is leaving and the dawn is coming when we see another person and know that he is our brother or she is our sister. Otherwise, no matter the hour, it is still dark.

Things have changed in Jackson; community power is now shared by people of every hue under the leadership of a black mayor. Power-sharing matters, you know, and surely negotiating community decisions together is an important step toward seeing each other as brother and sister.

If you ever doubt the power of Word of God, then remember what has happened in this nation over these years in large part through the faith and truth and beauty of the words of Dr. Martin Luther King, Jr. Exclusion and disdain for those different from ourselves still lurk in the human heart, which is why we need God so. But we are not as much in the darkness as we were. And God is not finished with us yet.

Earthly Good

Homemaking

Do not let your hearts be troubled. Believe in God, believe also in me. In my Father's house there are many dwelling places. If it were not so, would I have told you that I go to prepare a place for you? And if I go and prepare a place for you, I will come again and will take you to myself, so that where I am, there you may be also. John 14:1-3

Jesus said, Shh . . . peace. Don't be scared. Don't worry. It's going to be all right. Trust God. Trust me. We have a place just for you. I wouldn't lie to you. I'm showing you the way to get there. And I'm going to take you home.

Soft voice. Murmuring words. They must have loved the sound of the voice as much as the words. He'd made a home for them these years, even on the road. Here on this night, he had washed their feet and fed them supper, but then he said disturbing things about leaving them, about going away.

They were anxious, worried—he had been their homemaker. He'd hugged them and kidded them and made them laugh. He made their friends welcome and figured out how to feed all the extra company that showed up, a couple of times making a tiny mess of fish and a few measly loaves of bread go so far that it was like a miracle. When they went out, he was the one who reminded them to put on their cloaks and take their staffs and their sandals. He got mad at them when they were less than they could be; he hollered at them to put their swords up before they hurt somebody and he taught them how silly they were when they tried to one-up each other. He took them seriously and said they would do wonderful things. And he loved each one fiercely, and each one knew it. He was a homemaker.

He must have learned how to be a homemaker somewhere. How to make room for people, how to give them a safe place all their own. How to hold them close and gentle. How to feed them and heal their sore places. How to make them feel like they can do or be anything. It's very strange. Homemaking—when it's holy, when it's of God—doesn't make people who stay home. Holy homemaking makes people who can be at home anywhere and who will be strong enough to stride out into the vast world and become homemakers themselves for others.

Jesus must have learned some of this homemaking from his mother Mary, the one whose rhythms of blood and breath gave him his first songs. Her womb, her breast, her face had been home for him, full of grace, full of love. Her love had even been brave enough to let go of him. To start biting her lips and stop saying "be careful" as he grew up.

Surely it was her brave love and trust in God that let her boy loose to become who he was meant to be, to find his own way with strange friends and wild talk and frightening possibilities. And, of course, the worst did happen—a cross against the sky and her boy hanging on it and a sword piercing through her heart also. That's a perennial and terrible risk for a homemaker, even the most blessed among men and women. And yet we say, *Hail Mary, full of grace, the Lord is with thee. Blessed art thou among women and blessed is the fruit of thy womb, Jesus.*

But surely his deepest knowing of homemaking came from the heart of God, whose breath loved into being all that is. Who looked at the stars and alligators and butterflies and mountains and us and the universe and said, "This is really very good." Who loves it all, loves us all so much that God gave, well, you know the rest.

Perhaps the heart of Christian living is to begin—wherever, with whomever—to be homemakers. To hold our hearts open and roomy. To make room for the ones who do not seem at home in the world—the isolated, the alienated. To live as if we belong to one another and to God—because, of course, we do.

Earthly Good

I Once was Blind

There was a man born blind. Of course, he knows he's blind and so do his parents and the neighbors and all the church people. Everybody's comfortable with his blindness and he fits in fine. They probably feel sorry for him when they think about him. And every once in a while maybe they say 'there but for the grace of God' . . . . But mostly, he's just sort of there, part of the landscape.

The problems begin when Jesus shows up. Jesus doesn't go to see the priests or talk to the vestry or to the leaders in the town. Instead what he does is to see the blind man. Really see him. The disciples see him, too, and they want to know who's at fault here (which we still like to do). Jesus says, c'mon. Look deeper. Look for the glory of God. And Jesus spits on the ground and makes mud. And—somehow, in the spit and the dirt and the hands of the healer—somehow, in the mystery and power of humility, somehow, God says again: let there be light. And there was light.

And what is so strange is that when the story changes from the pitying of 'there but for the grace of God' to the miracle of 'there *is* the grace of God', nobody likes it. Nobody rejoices.

The neighbors say, This looks like a scam. Maybe this isn't even the same guy. And they take him to the preachers who say, This looks bad. We've got some rules broken here. How dare this stranger spit and make mud on the Sabbath. And how dare you go and get healed? And then the parents say, This looks like we could get into trouble. You're on your own, boy.

Nobody sees the grace of God going on here. No joy. No insight. No depth perception. Everybody just sees problems. Except the blind man who now just sees. Once I was blind. Now I see.

Isn't that strange? The blind one sees. And the seeing people have got so many blind spots, so little perspective. Because sometimes we forget that each of us only sees a little, and always from here or there or there, and only this little patch or that little squiggle. And mostly, we see through a glass darkly.

I know another man. This one was born sighted and strong and swift. A kid with a face born to charm, growing up with trophies and pretty girls and smiling pictures in the paper in the little New Jersey town where he lived. Then school's over: no more touchdowns or basketball goals. A little bored, a little lost. A wife, a child, jobs. Some growing up to do. More bored. More lost. So more and more drinking and a different kind of grass now and different white lines, too, and oblivion. Then his wife says 'no more' and he starts a kind of downward spiral landing in my old hometown, Atlanta. And the jobs come and go—all the money going to the dope man anyway. And he would wake up in the middle of another lost day and say, I cannot believe this is me. And he despised himself.

One night in the dark, two men beat him up. A steel-toed boot raised back, a whomp, a thud, crushing bone, eyesocket and eyeball. So much blood. We would not believe the blood, he said.

Days, then months, of pain and dark. Of course the doctors took the eye. He looked in the mirror and saw his smashed, sunken ruin of a face and decided that he didn't want to live. He was blind to any hope, any future. One thing he knew. Once he could see. And now, he was blind.

He wore a big black patch. The sun bothered his good eye in the day, and at night he had no depth perception, and poor equilibrium, so he was always stumbling in the dark. He hoped to die. He prayed to God either to return his sight or let him go home to God.

And, this is so strange, God did. Both. With blood and tears and prayer, in the power and mystery of humility, God said one more time: let there be light. And there was light. God brought to him day by day, month by month, people who could see grace for him. A longtime friend who had known that cocky, beautiful young boy running with such grace and could say to him, Now. I love you now. That was then and this is now and still I am here for you now. An old woman, seeing him hiding behind his patch in the store where he bagged groceries, and asking, Look at me, son. Can you tell which eye I am blind in? And my life is not over. And always his mother up in New Jersey and his brothers, voices saying Hold on. Hang on. We're praying for you. We pray for you to walk in the light.

And their prayers were answered. He landed in an addiction recovery program at my old parish. Sitting quiet with his patch like a mask for a couple of weeks. And they said, no need to cover up your blindness. We know about blindness. God knows we see enough of our own blindness. And he sat with that. Then they said, Okay, enough with the patch, enough with the mask: let's go get a glass eye. And he did. And a board member said, I think you look beautiful. Then, everybody bugging him to come out of that dark old room: C'mon and see everybody. C'mon, let everybody see you.

And by the grace of God, he's been coming out of that dark old room ever since. He wears glasses now, good looking steel rims and they set off a face of beauty deeper than charm. One day a stranger asked him for directions at the MARTA station, and he said, You know, you can tell when people look at you if they think something is wrong with you. And maybe then they look down at you or pity you. She just looked at me as if I am just a somebody. And I am.

When I asked him if I could tell his story he said yes and to tell you he can see. Not perfect. He sees imperfectly like you and me, which is why we all need each other so, for our blind spots and to find the insight. But he said to be sure and tell you this: that if you ever meet him, he hopes you will see a kind, gentle, loving person. He said to tell you, Thank God. And he said to tell that once he was blind. And now he can see.